NATION-BUILDING

Edited by

Karl W. Deutsch

and William J. Foltz

ALDINE • ATHERTON
chicago • new york

Foreword Copyright © 1966 by Atherton Press

Copyright © 1963 by Atherton Press

Manufactured in the United States of America
ISBN 0-202-24057-6
Library of Congress Catalog Card Number: 63-19788

Fourth Printing, 1971

Address all inquiries to:
Aldine·Atherton, Inc.
529 South Wabash Avenue
Chicago, Illinois 60605

The Study of Nation-Building, 1962-1966

FOREWORD

Karl W. Deutsch

It is typical of our time that it turns men from contemplation to action, and the sciences from theory to experiment. Astronomy and epistemology have taken on an increasingly experimental aspect in our age of spaceships and of machines steered by automatic light or heat receptors. Something similar has been happening to the study of society. Where in the past the formation and rise of nations were merely observed by scholars, today statesmen and voters increasingly want to *do* something about the process. They may want to establish or strengthen some national political entity of their own, or to merge it with or separate it from some other such entity. Or they may wish to strengthen, weaken, or otherwise change some other national political entity, so as to promote values and interests of their own.

In any case, they will not leave peoples and nations as they find them. Old empires are to be broken up, new nations made, and new federations or communities established. In the latter 1960s, we no longer discuss whether men can do these things.

We observe that they are doing them; and we know that they are likely to be doing even more along these lines in the future.

The Development of Research

Such increased action, in turn, evokes stronger responses on the part of political thinkers. The world over, our age is more political than any other, in concern as well as action; and it generates a growing body of new political theory in general, and of theories of political integration and political development in particular. These theories have given rise to an interest in ampler, more accurate data, which in turn have provided new criteria for the relevance and selection of further data. Both familiar production cycles of knowledge have thus been accelerated; the round from action and experience to theory and back to action, and the more scholarly or scientific round from theory to data and back to new theory, revised and verified and demanding still more data which in turn produce more theories. Despite the anxieties, the controversies, and the ideological conflicts of our time, the mounting thrust of this cumulative new knowledge is unmistakable.

The first impact of the new interest in research and theory has been a considerable expansion of our knowledge of cases of national and political evolution, particularly in the developing countries of the world. The study of these cases has been accompanied by efforts to interpret them. Many general collections of such studies appear in our bibliography of nation-building for 1963–1966. Here the collections edited by Gabriel Almond, Joseph La Palombara, Lucian Pye, K. H. Silvert, and Karl von Vorys stand out for the theoretical interests of their editors, as well as for the relevance of their materials and the quality of many of the individual contributions.[1] A double case study of Turkey and Japan, by Dankwart A. Rustow and Robert E. Ward, pursues fruitfully and in greater depth the theoretical interests of the group of Gabriel Almond and his collaborators in the study of political culture, communication and leadership in the modernizing process.[2]

Together with this wider knowledge of diverse cases have come more deeply probing questions of theory and the discovery or rediscovery of overlooked or neglected aspects of the nation-building process. Such broad theoretical questions are dealt with in David Apter's *Political Modernization* and in important articles by Harold Lasswell and by Samuel P. Huntington.[3] Specific new theoretical emphases include Louis Hartz' original and highly suggestive analysis of important common memories, culture patterns and political and intellectual traditions, tensions and conflicts in each of the "fragments" of European culture in such new overseas nations as the United States, Australia, Canada, and Argentina.[4] If Hartz compares relatively advanced new nations of Western culture with one another, Seymour Martin Lipset, in an unusually stimulating and fruitful analysis of the role of legitimacy and charismatic leadership in the forming of new nations, compares the United States of George Washington with the Ghana of Kwame Nkrumah—with startling but thought-provoking and highly penetrating conclusions.[5] A different and largely psychological approach to the study of common images is developed in a volume edited by Herbert Kelman; this, too, has important potential applications to the analysis of nation-building.[6]

Work on the theory of political integration has been carried on by Ernst B. Haas, by Amitai Etzioni, by Bruce M. Russett, and by the collaborators in a joint volume edited by Philip E. Jacob and James V. Toscano.[7]

The heightened interest in theories that can be verified and that lead to applications has led to an increased demand for quantitative political data—not any data, but data relevant to theories. The rapid development of better mathematical and statistical methods of analysis, and the increasing availability of electronic computing and data-processing equipment all have worked in the same direction. A volume on *Comparing Nations,* edited by Richard L. Merritt and Stein Rokkan, and two large analytic data surveys, one by Arthur S. Banks and Robert B. Textor and the other by Bruce M. Russett and his associates, are the first results of a new "data movement" that is now spreading on an international scale.[8]

The Development of New Nations

A great deal of all this research underscores a reality that is staring us in the face. At this time, the world of developing countries is becoming more rather than less nationalistic. In country after country, modernization moves people out of their villages and their traditions into the modern world of mobility, insecurity, need for political and governmental services, and formal or informal political participation. Everywhere in the world, this process of social mobilization makes the developing countries harder to govern by their own traditional elites, but still harder to govern from abroad. Everywhere the trend is toward rising costs of foreign intervention.

This is true of the Communist world no less than of the non-Communist countries. The Soviet Union could not control Yugoslavia after 1948, nor could it ever control Communist China. Nor, indeed, could Yugoslavia control Albania. Despite the international symbols of Communism, national states, national economies, and national decision systems have persisted wherever they had been well established at the level of popular images and habits.

Where no nation-state had been established, conditions have been different. With the possible exception of Outer Mongolia, no new nation-state has been created under Communism. In the non-Communist parts of the world, on the contrary, new nation-states have continued to come into existence. At present, the number of non-Communist states stands at over 120, and the movement toward government and sovereignty of many of the islands in the world's oceans is under way.[9]

The actual capacities of many of the new countries for self-government and for the maintenance of political cohesion have been quite limited. From the Congo to Laos and Viet Nam, political instability in many of the new countries has been extreme. In such countries only one form of rule seems even harder and more costly to maintain: government by foreigners.

In the long run, many of these countries may remain only loosely tied to any foreign power, large or small, near or far The effects of nationalism and distance that tend to preserve independence are likely to be enhanced by those of preindustrial inefficiency as well as by the national self-preoccupation that goes with most national efforts to industrialize. In what symbolic language these new countries and peoples are likely to express their persistent national separateness—whether in the imagery of Karl Marx, Thomas Jefferson, Kemal Atatürk, or Mahatma Gandhi—may make little difference in practice to their persistent desire to give far less to any international coalition or alliance than they expect to get from it. What they have to give—and it may not be ample—they are most likely to give to their own development.

Even then, some of the new countries may not stay in one piece. To speak of a single "indivisible" nation, and to speak of "territorial integrity" as of paramount importance in countries where loyalties are fluid and national unity may not in fact exist—this is to let rhetoric obscure reality. If governments increasingly depend on the consent of the governed for most of their powers, just or not, so do nations increasingly depend on that same consent for their cohesion.

Where this consent is lacking, and where there are no conditions for its early development, even a new nation, recently split off from a larger empire, may be likely to split into still further fragments. Finding the size for any state at which it will be cohesive and stable is in part a process of historical trial and error. If it should be large enough to be economically viable, it should also be small enough to be governed effectively by a government that is close to the people, that is responsive to its needs, and that is in turn supported by it.

In recent years, these pressures toward smallness of countries seem to have been somewhat more powerful than the pressures toward greater size. Few, if any, of the world's small new countries at early stages of economic development have during that time lost their independence for lack of economic viability. On the contrary, cases in which larger political units or federations have broken up have been many and conspicuous: the Mali Federation, the British West Indies Federation, the British Central African Federation, the expulsion of Singapore from Malaysia, the secession of Syria from the United Arab Republic, and the continued strife between the Greek and Turkish inhabitants of Cyprus all come readily to mind.

Thus the art of nation-building in the next few years may to a considerable extent depend on the art of nation-limiting. This would be the art of persuading new nations to limit themselves to a size manageable for their own integrative and decision-making capabilities, as well as the art of separating populations and territories wherever too many people seem to be imprisoned in hardened deadlocks of mutual frustration and rising resentment. Agreeing to differ, two or several such new nations may then become good friends.

If new states have multiplied, including many small ones, the larger powers have not abandoned the substance of nationalism and national self-preoccupation. Under De Gaulle, France has openly invoked the symbols of national grandeur. The German Federal Republic has emphasized its intense concern with the national reunification of divided Germany. The largest powers, however—the United States, the Soviet Union and Communist China—have tended to represent to themselves and to others their national viewpoints and desires in the garb of international symbols and a worldwide mission. It could almost be said that there were two kinds of nationalist powers in the mid-1960s: those who knew that they were nationalists, and those who did not.

In the latter 1960s ignorance of the limitations of their own outlook and of their limited ability to control events threatened great and small powers alike. Major sustained efforts were needed to keep the world from sliding into an age of national destruction, and to keep open the path to a future in which nation-building could continue.

NOTES

[1] Gabriel A. Almond and Lucian W. Pye, eds. *Comparative Political Culture.* Princeton: Princeton University Press, 1965; Joseph La Palombara, ed. *Bureaucracy and Political Development.* Princeton: Princeton University Press, 1963; Lucian W. Pye, ed. *Communication and Political Development.* Princeton: Princeton University Press, 1963; K. H. Silvert, ed. *Expectant Peoples: Nationalism and Development.* New York: Random House, 1963; Karl von Vorys, ed. "New Nations: The Problem of Political Development." *The Annals of the American Academy of Political and Social Science,* March 1965.

[2] Dankwart A. Rustow and Robert E. Ward, eds. *Turkey and Japan: A Comparative Study of Modernization.* Princeton: Princeton University Press, 1964.

[3] David E. Apter. *The Politics of Modernization.* Chicago: University of Chicago Press, 1965; Harold D. Lasswell. "The Policy Sciences of Development": Review Article. *World Politics,* January 1965; Samuel P. Huntington. "Political Development and Political Decay." *World Politics,* April 1965.

[4] Louis Hartz. *The Founding of New Societies: Studies in the History of the United States, Latin America, South Africa, Canada and Australia.* With contributions by Kenneth D. McRae and others. New York: Harcourt, Brace & World, 1964.

[5] Seymour Martin Lipset. *The First New Nation: The United States in Historical and Comparative Perspective.* New York: Basic Books, 1963.

[6] Herbert Kelman, ed. *International Behavior: A Social-Psychological Analysis.* New York: Holt, Rinehart & Winston, 1965.

[7] Ernst B. Haas. *Beyond the Nation-State: Functionalism and International Organization.* Stanford: Stanford University Press, 1964. Especially Chapter 14, "Functionalism, Nationalism and Historical Sociology," pp. 459–497; Amitai Etzioni. *Political Unification: A Comparative Study of Leaders and Forces.* New York: Holt, Rinehart & Winston, 1965; Bruce M. Russett. *Community and Contention: Britain and America in the Twentieth Century.* Cambridge: M.I.T. Press, 1963. Especially Chapter 12, "Notes on a Theory of Integration," pp. 208–221; Philip E. Jacob and James V. Toscano, eds. *The Integration of Political Communities.* Philadelphia: Lippincott, 1964.

[8] Richard L. Merritt and Stein Rokkan, eds. *Comparing Nations: The Use of Quantitative Data in Cross-national Research.* New Haven: Yale University Press, 1965; Arthur S. Banks and Robert B. Textor. *A Cross-Polity Survey.* Cambridge: M.I.T. Press, 1963; Bruce M. Russett, *et al. World Handbook of Political and Social Indicators.* New Haven: Yale University Press, 1964.

[9] A list of data for 141 countries is given in an Appendix to the revised edition of my *Nationalism and Social Communication,* Cambridge, M.I.T. Press, 1966.

PREFACE

This book grew out of a panel discussion at the September, 1962, meeting of The American Political Science Association. The panel sought to bring together and compare the views and findings of scholars examining the formation of nations in various parts of the world and at various historical periods. Through the kind cooperation of The American Political Science Association and of Atherton Press, the fruits of this discussion, augmented by the contributions of Hermann Weilenmann and Richard L. Merritt and a bibliography by Donald J. Puchala, are here presented.

Grateful thanks are given the Carnegie Corporation for its support of the part of the research on which the Introduction and Chapter 4 are based, to Anna Merritt for preparing the index, and to Elizabeth M. Baskin for carefully typing the manuscript.

Karl W. Deutsch
William J. Foltz

New Haven, Connecticut
June 1963

CONTENTS

CONTRIBUTORS

Karl W. Deutsch is professor of political science at Yale University. His previous books include *Nationalism and Social Communication* (1953), *An Interdisciplinary Bibliography of Nationalism* (1956), and *The Nerves of Government* (1963). He is co-author of *Germany Rejoins the Powers* (1959), *Political Community in the North Atlantic Area* (1957), and *Modern Political Systems, Europe* (1963).

Rupert Emerson is professor of government and research associate at the Center for International Affairs, Harvard University. His books include *Malaysia* (1937), *Representative Government in South East Asia* (1955), and *From Empire to Nation* (1960).

William J. Foltz is assistant professor of political science at Yale University. His writings include a forthcoming book, *From French West Africa to the Mali Federation.*

Carl J. Friedrich is Eaton Professor of the Science of Government at Harvard University. His many books include *Constitutional Government and Democracy* (1941), *The New Belief in the Common Man* (1942), *Inevitable Peace* (1947), *The Age of the Baroque* (1953), *The Philosophy of Law in Historical Perspective* (1958), and *Man and His Government* (1963). He is co-author of *Studies in Federalism* (1954) and *Totalitarian Dictatorship and Autocracy* (1956).

Richard L. Merritt is assistant professor of political science at Yale University. His writings include a forthcoming book, *Symbols of American Community, 1735–1775.*

Robert E. Scott is professor of political science at the University of Illinois. He is the author of *Mexican Government in Transition* (1959).

Joseph R. Strayer is Dayton-Stockton Professor of History at Princeton University. He is a former vicepresident of the Mediaeval Academy of America and is the author of *The Administration of Normandy under St. Louis* (1932), *Studies in Early French Taxation* (1939), *Western Europe in the Middle Ages* (1954), and co-author of *Feudalism in History* (1956).

Donald J. Puchala is an assistant in instruction at Yale University.

Hermann Weilenmann, director of the People's University of the Canton of Zurich, is a leading Swiss authority on civic education and language problems. His books include *Die vielsprachige Schweiz* (1925), *Der Zusammenschluss der Eidgenossenschaft* (1940), and *Pax Helvetica* (1950).

David A. Wilson is associate professor of political science at the University of California, Los Angeles, and a consultant to the RAND Corporation. He is the author of *Politics in Thailand* (1962).

Nation-Building and National Development: Some Issues for Political Research

INTRODUCTION

Karl W. Deutsch

How and when do nations come into existence, how and when do they pass away, and how and when can men decide the outcome by their actions?

We know that mankind existed long before nations, and we have good reason to hope that mankind will exist long after them. The era of nations and nationalism is a short span in recorded history, but in various parts of the world this age of nations— everywhere succeeding ages of villages, tribes, and empires—has begun at different times.

Scholars who have studied mainly a single geographic or cultural area have been tempted to see the rise of nationalism and of nations in that area either as something alien or as something unique and peculiar to the area. Investigators, however, who have paid careful attention to more than one country or area—and particularly those who have compared the long history of nationalism in Europe with its shorter histories in Latin America, Asia, and Africa—have soon discovered the intellectual power that is inherent in such comparisons. They have discovered that the making and breaking of nations is a process that is now occurring in most parts of the world and that it is a process which must be studied in its general and uniform aspects, especially if the unique features of each country and epoch are eventually to be understood better than they have been thus far.

The essays in this book are early steps in the comparison and analysis across the continents and centuries. To some degree, each of them combines three concerns: the concerns of the historian, the concern of the social scientist, and the concern of the policy-maker and statesman.

The descriptive and analytical scholar begins with the organized complexity of something that stands visibly before him; the historian deals with processes the outcomes of which are known.[1] Both use their knowledge of general regularities of social processes mainly to understand better the unique configuration of repetitive factors that makes up the particular contemporary institution or past sequence of events with which they are concerned. Historians thus use their knowledge of many general regularities in order to understand a few situations. Social scientists work mainly in the opposite direction: they start from a multitude of particular and seemingly unique facts and then search for general rules that can be derived from them. They study many situations to discover a few regularities. Put into somewhat more modern terms, social scientists often study the distribution of events and the information that can be gained from comparing differing distribution patterns. Policy-makers and statesmen, finally, use both their knowledge of general regularities and their judgment of partially unique situations in order to influence many specific outcomes in the direction of their general values.

Each of these viewpoints tends to favor a somewhat different

[1] For an extremely stimulating discussion of certain aspects of the historian's approach, see Leonard Krieger, "The Horizons of History," *American Historical Review*, 53, No. 1 (1957), 62–74; and William L. Langer, "The Next Assignment," *ibid.*, No. 2 (1958), 283–304.

perception of the problems of nationalism and of the rise and fall of nations. Many historians speak of the "growth of nations"; some historians and many statesmen and policy-oriented political scientists speak of "nation-building"; many social scientists prefer to think and speak of "national development."

Each of these images, however, carries its own cognitive implications which may reach beyond the motives for which the image was originally chosen. "National growth" suggests an organismic image, the growth of a living thing that cannot be dissected without injuring or killing it and, moreover, a growth process that is expected to pass through certain fixed intervals of time and through certain fixed qualitative stages toward a maturity the form of which is known and beyond which there are only decline and death or reproduction which starts a new, but essentially identical, cycle.

"Nation-building," by contrast, suggests an architectural or mechanical model. As a house can be built from timber, bricks, and mortar, in different patterns, quickly or slowly, through different sequences of assembly, in partial independence from its setting, and according to the choice, will, and power of its builders, so a nation can be built according to different plans, from various materials, rapidly or gradually, by different sequences of steps, and in partial independence from its environment.

Finally, the concept of "national development" also implies a limited but significant degree of combinatorial freedom. It is reminiscent of the mechanistic and voluntaristic aspects of the "nation-building" concept, but it also includes an awareness of internal and external interdependence in both space and time. This awareness characterizes the organismic image and tends to stress the influence of the past, the environment, and the vast, complex, and slow-changing aspects of the actions and expectations of millions of people. These actions and expectations limit the speed and scope of "nation-building" while offering significant opportunities and choices and strategic decision points for possible intervention and partial control.

These conceptual problems are made visible in the chapters

by Joseph Strayer and Carl Friedrich. The combinatorial aspects of the process of national development and the choice of national alignment are illustrated in the chapters by Hermann Weilenmann and Richard Merritt. Important missing links in the Latin American process are stressed by Robert Scott. The power of political manipulation, combined at a critical point with an ongoing social upheaval which accelerates and channels its energies, is described in the revolutionary wars of Asia by David Wilson. The vexing policy problems of Africa—problems that might be further illuminated by an explicit, critical choice and discussion of the conceptual models used—are presented by Rupert Emerson and William Foltz. Many other issues of nation-building and national development are illuminated by the implied dialogues and debates among our various chapters.

How and when do nations break away from larger political units, and how do they triumph over smaller units, such as tribes, castes, or local states, and more or less integrate them into the political body of the nation?

Here our chapters point to much unfinished business for research. What exactly is a tribe, and just what is meant by "tribalism"? How uniform a meaning can be attributed to these terms, which are so freely used in political discourse? Anthropologists sometimes call a tribe that social and political unit which is above the kin group and is still small enough to claim common descent although it is large enough to permit intermarriage. This definition is neither rigorous nor uniform, but the variety of groups called "tribes" is still larger, and the political use of the terms "tribe" and "tribalism" is still looser. Nevertheless, even the loose terms refer to real groups and problems, and the accounts by Strayer, Friedrich, and Weilenmann of the eventual overcoming of tribalism in medieval and early modern Europe may shed some light on the partly analogous contemporary problems in Africa discussed by Emerson and Foltz.

Similar considerations apply to the time and size dimensions of each major tribe. How old is it? How quickly was it formed and from what elements? How long would it be likely to endure under various conditions? Tribes, we know from European history, can change their language and culture; they can absorb other tribes; and large tribes came into existence through federation or mergers of smaller tribes or through their conquest and absorption by a larger one.[2]

In contrast to this picture of plasticity and change, many writings on African and Asian politics still seem to treat tribes as fixed and unlikely to change in any significant way during the next decades. Yet in contemporary Asia and Africa, the rates of cultural and ethnic change, although still low, are likely to be faster than they were in early medieval Europe. Press reports from the former Belgian Congo in 1961 mentioned that 26 per cent of natives were free from the (tribal) customary way of life, as against only about 12 per cent a generation earlier. Research is needed to establish more reliable figures, but it seems likely from the experience of ethnic minorities in other parts of the world that the process of partial modernization will draw many of the most gifted and energetic individuals into the cities or the growing sectors of the economy away from their former minority or tribal groups, leaving these traditional groups weaker, more stagnant, and easier to govern.

Research on the speed, scope, and quality of change among the tribes and within them also requires more attention to the relative size and manpower of these tribes. The distribution curve of tribes and ethnic or linguistic groups, ranked by their numerical strength, usually shows a few relatively strong languages or groups—perhaps six—which among them comprise more than half the total population of the territory. About ten to fifteen languages or groups are then likely to include over 90 per cent of the population, and the dozens or hundreds of remaining petty tribes or language groups are likely to add up to less than one-

---

[2] For the old Saxon tribe in northwestern Germany between 450 and 750 see, for example, Rudolf Buchner, "Germanentum und Papsttum von Chlodwig bis Pippin," in Fritz Valjavec, ed., *Historia Mundi* (Berne: Francke, 1956) V, *Frühes Mittelalter*, 161–162; and for the changes among the early Slavic tribes, George Vernadsky, "Das frühe Slawentum," *ibid.*, pp. 255–256, 275; for the changes in the barbarian war bands, tribes, or peoples in the territories of the former Roman Empire, see the thoughtful comment by Robert S. Lopez, *Naissance de l'Europe* (Paris: Armand Colin, 1962), pp. 39–40.

tenth of the population. Governments that can obtain the compliance or even the active support of a few of the largest groups —and thus usually of the majority of the population—then have a fair chance to maintain themselves in power over the entire territory of their state.

The dynamic processes of social mobilization and cultural assimilation—or, at least, of political integration even with continuing linguistic and cultural diversity—are thus likely to be more powerful in uniting or destroying an emerging people or a newly-established state than are the mere static facts of the multiplicity of tribes or languages within its territory. To assess these processes, however, richer data and more detailed studies will be needed.

Detailed studies of national integration will also pose a challenge to analysis. Just what do we mean when we say that "tribalism" or any other social and political attachment to a small ethnic, cultural, or linguistic group has been "overcome" in the process of national integration?

Tribes or other smaller ethnic or cultural groups could be politically related to the state and the nation in several ways. They may flatly deny membership in the nation, refuse obedience to the state, and rise in war against other groups of those who are officially supposed to be their fellow citizens. If they are less hostile or less self-confident, they may passively obey the government and comply with its demands as long as they are being supervised more-or-less directly by government officials and soldiers, but they may rise against the state in times of crisis in order to secede. In that event, they will already be a source of taxes and manpower for some national purposes but they still will require garrisons of national troops whose presence in these districts of the amalgamated national state will express the latent danger of civil war and the continued lack of integration.

If the members of the tribe or minority group have become more reconciled to their inclusion in the state, they may no longer be likely to rise in times of crisis and thus no longer require any garrisons from the rest of the state, but they might still lift no finger to aid the nation in its hour of need. Tribes or minor-

6

ities in such a situation already may be called not only politically amalgamated under the common government of the national state but also integrated from the viewpoint of military security, since they—like any sovereign but reliably non-hostile state—pose no active military threat against which any significant military resources would have to be committed.

If the political integration of such tribes or minorities has gone beyond this minimum, however, the state may then count on their "good citizenship"—that is, on their unsupervised compliance in most situations and on their active support in case of need—even though they may have preserved their ethnic, cultural, or linguistic distinctness and their reluctance to condone intermarriage or to engage in close social or personal relations across the boundaries of their group. In terms of political loyalty, all the diverse groups may be integrated solidly and dependably into a single nation or united in one amalgamated national state, federal or unitary. In terms of habits of communication, their cultures may have become sufficiently similar to let them communicate and act together as one people, but their ethnic, linguistic, or other group diversity still has been preserved as it has been preserved among the Englishmen, Welshmen, and Scotsmen that have for centuries made up the British people and the British nation or among the four language groups that have made the Swiss people and the Swiss nation.

Finally, these diverse groups within the same state—and by now within the same people and nation—may become wholly assimilated to the majority of their countrymen in language, culture, probabilities of intermarriage, and close personal relations until they have become indistinguishable as a group.

Open or latent resistance to political amalgamation into a common national state; minimal integration to the point of passive compliance with the orders of such an amalgamated government; deeper political integration to the point of active support for such a common state but with continuing ethnic or cultural group cohesion and diversity; and, finally, the coincidence of political amalgamation and integration with the assimilation of all groups to a common language and culture—these could be the main stages on the way from tribes to nation.[3] Since a nation is not an animal or vegetable organism, its evolution need not go through any fixed sequence of these steps.

Linguistic assimilation may long have preceded the amalgamation into a single state, as it did in the unification of Germany and Italy; political integration likewise may develop well before the ultimate decision-making powers of several governments are amalgamated into one, as Richard Merritt's chapter shows for the American colonies. Yet the most frequent sequence in modern Asia and Africa may well be the one sketched above. How long might it take for tribes or other ethnic groups in a developing country to pass through some such sequence of stages? We do not know, but European history offers at least a few suggestions. In the forcible incorporation of the Saxons into the Frankish empire and their forcible conversion to the Christian religion and culture, the period of open violence lasted thirty-two years, from 772 to 804; and it took more than another century, until 919, for a Saxon prince to don Frankish dress to ascend, as Henry I, the throne of the empire and to symbolize the active integration of his people into the common state.[4]

The speech of Saxons and Franks, though not identical, had been mutually intelligible to a considerable extent. Nevertheless, the assimilation of the two large tribes or peoples in regard to culture and speech did not occur for many centuries. More than five centuries later, several separate translations of the Bible had to be made—one into High German, the standard language gradually being adopted by the descendants of the Franks near Frank-

---

[3] For more detailed discussion of these concepts, see Karl W. Deutsch, *Nationalism and Social Communication* (New York: Wiley, 1953); *idem, Political Community at the International Level* (Garden City, New York: Doubleday, 1954); *idem et al., Political Community and the North Atlantic Area* (Princeton: Princeton University Press, 1957); *idem, Backgrounds for Community* (forthcoming).

[4] See Gerd Tellenbach, "Europa im Zeitalter der Karolinger" in Valjavec, *op. cit.,* p. 406; Paul Kirn, "Das Abendland vom Ausgang der Antike bis zum Zerfall des Karolingischen Reiches," in Walter Goetz, ed., *Propyläen-Weltgeschichte,* III, *Das Mittelalter bis zum Ausgang der Staufer* (Berlin: Propyläen-Verlag, 1932), 106–108, 124; Karl Hampe, "Abendländisches Hochmittelalter," *ibid.,* pp. 301–303.

furt and in Southern Germany; another into Low German, the standard language derived from the speech of the Saxons; and a third into Dutch, the standard language derived from the Low Frankish speech of the populations which in 1648 finally seceded from the empire to become the Dutch nation.[5] Smaller linguistic minorities, more interspersed or intermingled with the settlements of other populations, were assimilated in medieval Europe within a time of between one hundred and four hundred years. These were the approximate time spans for the linguistic assimilation of the Langobards in Italy (568–c. 750), of the Scandinavian-speaking Normans in Normandy (955–c. 1050), and later of the French-speaking Normans in England (1066–c. 1400). Modern immigrant populations, particularly in cities, have tended to assimilate much faster, often within twenty to fifty years, at least in situations where there were social, economic, and cultural incentives to assimilation, as usually was the case in North and South America.

Generally, the political pacification and the establishment of minimal compliance have preceded by far the assimilation of minorities; minorities have often continued to express their particular patterns of social cohesion and political preference within the framework of a common state without necessarily threatening its continued existence. In the case of majority populations, there is often the opposite pattern: a certain amount of social and cultural assimilation—or, at least, compatibility—may have to be established first if a common political regime is to endure.

The chapters in this volume offer fascinating illustrations of these points and of the diversity of possible patterns and their interpretation in various parts of the world. William J. Foltz expresses doubts as to whether the skills and habits of political participation can be taught to African populations within a few generations; David Wilson reports how, under the auspices of a dictatorial ideology and in the crucible of revolutionary war, such skills are being taught to large numbers of Asians; and

[5] For references, see the literature cited in Deutsch, "The Trend of European Nationalism: The Language Aspect," *American Political Science Review*, XXXVI, No. 3 (1942), 533–541.

Robert Scott points out how even a considerable level of economic modernization and mass communication may fail to produce effective mass participation, responsibility, and loyalty in Latin American politics as long as the elusive but crucial problems of identity and congruity are not being solved.

On these points the European experience may have some relevance. Carl Friedrich notes that the power of kings and other rulers is not an uncaused cause. Nation-building, he suggests, is "a matter of building group cohesion and group loyalty for international representation and domestic planning." How and why are some governments, elites, and policies more successful in attracting support for this undertaking and in evoking loyalties than are their rivals? Who becomes loyal to a group, a tribe, or a nation—when and why? Based on a long study of history as well as much experience in the political and educational practice of nation-building from highly diverse elements in the Swiss democracy, Weilenmann's chapter condenses a great amount of knowledge on this point. What appears as a process of nation-building from the point of view of governments here appears as a matter of nation-choosing by the individual. As Weilenmann sees it, it is an act of personal choice, or rather a sequence of choices, made in terms of the needs inherent in an individual's personality as well as in his external situation. Both personality and situation may be changed to some extent and made and remade by the consequences of each choice. This is almost an existential view of nationality, for it goes well beyond the demand for law and order mentioned by Strayer, and it is, perhaps, a realistic view that might be fruitfully applied to the problems of national integration in other parts of the world and that might be advantageously combined with the results of other studies of personality and politics.[6]

The choice of national alignments and national identity is

---

[6] See, for example, Erik H. Erikson, *Childhood and Society* (New York: Norton, 1950); *idem, Young Man Luther, A Study of Psychoanalysis and History* (New York: Norton, 1958); Lucian W. Pye, *Chinese Guerrilla Communism in Malaya, Its Social and Political Meaning* (Princeton: Princeton University Press, 1956); *idem, Politics, Personality and Nation-Building: Burma's Search for Identity* (New Haven: Yale University Press, 1962); and *idem,* "Personal

related to the decision to choose a common enemy. This is indeed a decision, even if it has been made unconsciously. Carl Friedrich refers to the Spanish people as having become united in their "struggle against the Arab overlords." Why did they choose to struggle rather than to submit? No such unifying struggles took place at such other boundaries of Islam—or of the Arab language area—as the Sudan, Morocco, Mesopotamia, or India; to see the Arabs as overlords to be resisted was in part a response to a situation of social stratification, but in part it was a decision that changed the destiny of those who took it.

Similar questions are now acute in Asia and Africa. Whom will the populations there choose to consider their common enemy at each particular time and place, and whom will they choose as their allies? In response to what conditions and existential needs will they make their choices in each case and with what consequences for their own identity? We can say something about the conditions: usually two groups must have something important in common before they are likely to consider a new intruder as a "common enemy" rather than as an ally and to see each other as allies rather than as enemies. But, even if we know the initial conditions well, a crucial element of arbitrary choice quite often will remain.

It is with such considerations in mind that we may come to appreciate the thoughtful definition of a nation proposed by Carl Friedrich. Spelled out in greater detail, his definition, if I have understood it correctly, seems to imply at least five major points. A nation, in his view, is any sizable population or group of persons which can be called:

> *independent,* in the sense that it is not ruled from outside;

> *cohesive,* by virtue of its markedly more effective habits of easy and varied social communication and cooperation, compared with their corresponding capa-

---

Identity and Political Ideology," *Behavioral Science,* 6, No. 3 (1961), 205–221; and Daniel Lerner, *The Passing of Traditional Society* (Glencoe, Ill.: Free Press, 1958).

bilities and motivations for communication and co-operation with outsiders;

politically organized, in the sense that it provides a constituency for a government which exercises effective rule within it;

autonomous, in that it accords to this government such acclaim, consent, compliance, and support as to make its rule effective;

internally legitimate, in the sense that its habits of compliance with and support of the government, or, at least, toward mutual political cooperation and membership in the nation, are connected with broader beliefs about the universe and about their own nature, personalities, and culture so that their support for the nation, even in times of adversity, is likely and thus ensures its endurance. (This internal legitimacy, anchored in the beliefs of its own population, may be largely independent of the opinions of other populations or of foreign governments.)

This definition does much to bring together a great deal that has been learned and thought about the nature and development of nations. It could be applied to further comparative research on the emerging nations of Asia and Africa, as well as to Friedrich's fascinating question about whether a European nation might be in process of emergence in the 1960's.

If Friedrich deepens and clarifies the concept of an emerging nation, Merritt demonstrates the usefulness of verifiable quantitative data for the study of such questions. When we have comparable data for other periods and other parts of the world—such data as are now beginning to be collected by the Yale Political Data Program [7]—and if we have scholars inter-

---

[7] For a brief description, see Karl W. Deutsch, Harold D. Lasswell, Richard L. Merritt, and Bruce M. Russett, *The Yale Political Data Program* ("Yale Papers in Political Science," 4 [New Haven: Yale University Political Science Research Library, 1963]).

preting them with care and perception, we shall know a good deal more about the building of nations.

Scott notes the limits of quantitative data. Weilenmann suggests that men choose groups and nations in answer to their needs and that groups and nations derive their strength from their ability to attract and consolidate such choices; Scott suggests the corollary to this view—the failure of this need-fulfilling, need-combining, and need-consolidating function and the failure to create sufficient identity and congruity in the relations of nation, government, and individual may be key elements in what Scott sees as the failure of national integration in Latin America. There, as he reports, quantitative indexes of social mobilization would suggest opportunities for far greater progress toward nationhood than seems to have been attained in political practice. His chapter is a reminder that economic and social change does not automatically create loyalties and institutions, but, at best, gives men opportunities for their creation and that here, too, the presence or absence of concomitant cultural and moral changes may be crucial.

Wilson illustrates the possibilities of one process—the pattern of revolutionary war that has characterized nationalistic and communist movements in much of eastern Asia—of concomitant cultural, political, and military change. Carried to its extreme by the Communists, the attempt to combine nationalistic appeal and military effort with a policy of far-reaching cultural, social, and economic change has also been used in only somewhat more moderate form by many non-communist regimes. Here again, a comparison with the outcome of revolutionary war in the history of other parts of the world might throw some light on the potentialities and limits of the process.

The final chapters, by Emerson and Foltz, illustrate the problems of applying our very incomplete knowledge of nation-building and national development to sub-Sahara Africa. Emerson writes with insight, wisdom, skepticism, and compassion, recalling the many unsolved problems in evaluating the present and prospective strength of nationalism in Africa. Foltz raises intriguing problems on the contrast between confident African nationalistic expectations and skeptical Western perspectives.

13

KARL W. DEUTSCH

The two chapters on Africa point to potentially fruitful lines of research. Emerson raises the whole problem of the persistent or transitory nature of tribal minorities and of the differing but not unrelated rates of political integration and ethnic assimilation—the two rates which may make the difference between a pattern of civil war, as in Algeria, and a pattern of peaceful ethnic bargaining, as in the "balanced ticket" of New York City politics. His chapter suggests the need for better research on the actual numerical strength of all the various minority tribes and languages, on the number and rates of growth of partially or wholly detribalized populations, and on the prospects of building more powerful and stable political coalitions from some of these variegated elements.

Emerson also notes the imperfectly understood problem of African boundaries. Which ones are "natural," and which ones "unnatural"? Who seems likely to spend how much effort on attempts to change them? To my knowledge, no careful general study of African boundaries has been made, nor has there been a probing comparison between African boundaries and comparable boundaries in Asia and Latin America—a scholarly enterprise in which the resources of geography, history, political science, and sociology might have to be combined.[8]

Professor Foltz highlights another problem for research: the current scarcity of high-school–educated, "middle-level," elite groups in many parts of Africa and the resulting cleavages between a very small upper layer of university-educated Africans, often with European or American training, and the large mass of their uneducated or poorly educated countrymen. According to Foltz, in the old elite families there is a related cleavage between the small minority of young foreign-trained and technically

[8] For a beginning in this direction, see George P. Murdock, *Africa: Its Peoples and Their Culture History* (New York: McGraw-Hill, 1959); S. B. Jones, *Boundary-Making: A Handbook for Statesmen, Treaty Editors and Boundary Commissioners* (Washington: Carnegie Endowment for International Peace, 1945); S. W. Boggs, *International Boundaries* (New York: Columbia University Press, 1940); Karl Haushofer, *Grenzen in ihrer geographischen und politischen Bedeutung* (Heidelberg: Vowinckel, 1939); D. Whittlesey, *The Earth and State: A Study of Political Geography* (New York: Holt, 1939).

competent elite members and the older and less well-trained fathers, brothers, or other relatives. He notes the need for broader and deeper studies of African elite recruitment and of the probable changes in the composition of future African elites. African parties are likely to require increasingly the services of local and district functionaries, many of whom will not be rich, foreign trained, or university educated. Labor unions and rural cooperatives are likely to elevate to local and regional leadership a similar elite of urban or rural lower- or lower middle-class origin who have only an elementary or, at most, a high-school education. Any progress in industrialization or economic development will similarly demand expansion in secondary school training. Any gains in literacy will swell the demand for elementary school teachers in towns and villages, and the newly literate young adults may soon furnish a public for mass publication on a relatively low cultural level, resembling the "penny press," tabloids, pulp magazines, and comic strips and catering to similar recently acculturated strata in Europe, America, and, perhaps, India.[9] All this may mean the gradual shift in many African states to a new elite with less formal education and more intensely national experience, backed by a similar, widening public for the mass media and for increasingly sustained political participation.

Another set of issues raised by Foltz has wider implications for Africa. He mentions the exploitation of the peasants by the new national states and governments and the frequent lack of appreciation by the latter of any possible economic benefits that might flow from an expansion of their countries' private economic sectors, either native-owned or foreign. Experts from the former colonial administrations, as well as spokesmen for Western business groups or settlers, have often stressed these points. Perhaps just as often, African and Asian nationalists have done the exact contrary, minimizing the economic pressure of the new nationalist governments on the rural population and predominantly casting private business interests in the role of the ex-

[9] For a discussion of this problem in India, see Selig S. Harrison, *India, the Most Dangerous Decades* (Princeton: Princeton University Press, 1960).

ploiter. It seems hardly plausible that in this debate all the truth should be on one side, but to ascertain how much truth there is in which claim and under what conditions will require a combination of skilled political and economic research.

There are many ways to read this book. We may note how the discussion moves from the general to the specific. The chapters dealing with Europe, where the political and historical evidence is richest and where the nation-building period most often seems distant in time, tend to be most abstract and to stress the broadest outlines of the nation-making process. The discussion is only somewhat less abstractly conceived; the chapter on Asia concentrates on one process, that of revolutionary war; the two chapters on Africa, where the creation or failure of nation-states is a matter of the political here and now, raise the largest number of concrete problems. Each of these approaches is worth pursuing; taken together, they may mean more than each of them could singly. There are many other aspects on which interest might center, but these, too, are likely to show how much each of the chapters can contribute to a deeper understanding of the others.

In many ways, these chapters make a book that is not finished, yet it is a book that is more than the sum of its parts. It suggests the opportunities for insight that come from the comparison of cases and the dialogue of scholars. Neither this book nor this dialogue will be properly finished until much more is known about the complexities of the topic. Yet, even as an expression of the incompleteness of our knowledge, it may suggest by how much our knowledge has grown in recent years and what real promise it holds of increasing in the future.

The Historical
Experience
of Nation-Building
in Europe

I

Joseph R. Strayer

The roots of modern European states go back to the barbarian
regna which arose in the period of the collapse of the Roman
Empire and the concomitant migration of peoples. I am using
the Latin term for these units because the English word "kingdom" carries too many overtones of an organized state. The barbarian *regnum* was certainly not a state, although it is rather
difficult to say just what it was. Though the ruler often took an
ethnic title (*rex Anglorum, rex Francorum,* and so on), most of
the *regna* were not ethnic units. The usual pattern was a dominant warrior group, drawn from several Germanic peoples, ruling a subject population which was Latin, Celtic, or Slav. To
take the most famous example, the Franks were themselves a
federation of peoples; they conquered and gradually merged
with other Germanic groups, such as the Burgundians and the
Alemanni; they ruled Romanized Gauls, Italians, Celtic refugees
from Britain, and a certain number of Slavs. It is clear that such
a *regnum* could not be a cultural unit any more than it was an

ethnic unit—there were always many dialects, frequently many languages, always different customs, and usually different laws for each of the constituent groups. Even geography does not help much, for a *regnum* was only roughly a geographical unit. It might have had a core, but it would be hard to define its boundaries—there were, everywhere, contested districts and loosely attached, more or less autonomous dependencies (e.g., Aquitaine for the Franks, Wales for the Anglo-Saxons).

Thus, a *regnum* had to be defined in terms of its king, or better, its royal family. A *regnum* was made up of the people who recognized a certain family as *their* royal family. This group may have fluctuated in size and the territories which it occupied, but as long as a sizable number of people held a certain man to be their king, a *regnum* existed.

These *regna* were amorphous and, at first, ephemeral. Yet, some of them survived and, merely by surviving, took the first step in nation-building. Very slowly, very gradually, they built up a persisting identity. Certain peoples, occupying certain areas, long constituted and were, therefore, expected to go on constituting, a certain *regnum*. And, because their *regnum* endured for many generations, there began to be a feeling that it was a permanent part of the political landscape and that it should continue.

It is not surprising that the *regnum* had little resemblance to a state, for, in the early Middle Ages, it is doubtful that anyone had a concept of a state. Some memory of the state lingered among the better-educated members of the clergy, but even they were not able to express the idea very clearly. Some kings, taught by the Church and, perhaps, by surviving Roman traditions, tried to preserve some of the governmental apparatus and public authority of a Roman emperor. Their efforts were frustrated. Most members of the ruling class had no idea of an impersonal continuing public power. Loyalty was to individuals or to families, not to the state. And even this personal loyalty was not wholly reliable; it was tested afresh every time there was a request for service or a demand for obedience. Political power more and more entered the domain of private law; it was a personal possession which could be transmitted by marriage or divided among heirs. Being personal, political power was hard to exercise at a distance or through agents. Hence, there was a constant tendency for local representatives of the king to become independent rulers, a tendency aggravated by the low level of economic activity, which made each district almost self-sufficient. All these factors—the emphasis on personal loyalty, the treatment of public power as a private possession, and the tendency to local autonomy—existed long before feudalism became established. In fact, feudalism was simply the recognition of an already existing political situation.

The process of building a state out of these unpromising materials took a long time, especially as it was done almost entirely with internal resources. The Byzantine model had little influence, and the Roman model was not very well known until the revival of legal studies in the twelfth century. By that time, some of the essential steps in state-building had already been accomplished.

The process seems to have been started by purely practical considerations. The mass of the population suffered from petty wars and general insecurity; it wanted more and better government, especially better administration of justice. This popular desire might have had little influence—after all, the people always want peace and seldom get it—but it was backed by the Church, then at the height of its power. Churchmen played important roles in every government and consistently taught that justice was the highest attribute of a king. They gave their prestige and their administrative skill to any effort to improve the administration of justice. Finally, the rulers themselves wanted to preserve and increase their political power and to hand it on unimpaired to their heirs. They found that the best way to do this was by trying to satisfy the popular demand for law and order. By suppressing violence, by forcing powerful men to settle their disputes through the courts, they gained a much greater degree of control over their vassals and subjects than they had ever had before. But to do this, rulers had to develop systems of law and regularly functioning courts. They had to get a monopoly of all the important cases for their courts or develop an effective appellate jurisdiction which could control the courts of their vassals. They had to create a corps of judges and administrators entirely dependent on them, men who could be rotated from district to district and office to office. And, in doing this, they had to create stable and enduring institutions. These institutions, built up in the late eleventh and twelfth centuries, became the nuclei around which states were formed.

While these institutions were developing, a great revival of learning took place. As a part of this revival, the logical, scientific, and political works of Aristotle were translated into Latin and the *Corpus Juris* of Justinian was studied with greater and greater intensity. Universities began to appear, and many university graduates became administrators and judges. A considerable number of teachers of law, philosophy, and theology began to speculate on political subjects. Out of this intellectual ferment, a theory of the state began to develop. It owed much to the revived study of Roman law, but it was not just a copy of Roman doctrines. Twelfth- and thirteenth-century scholars had to pay some attention to the political environment in which they lived, which was very different from that of Roman lawyers of the classical period. Thus, they had to consider problems of interstate relations, of Church-state relations, and of feudal or semifeudal relations— topics which had not been of any great importance in Roman law. Working with this mixture of old and new ingredients, medieval scholars developed a theory of the state which persisted, in its main outlines, well into the seventeenth century; that is, well past the period in which the European state-system became firmly established.

This theory, when it reached its full development at the end of the thirteenth century, contemplated a Europe divided into a number of sovereign states. The word "sovereignty" had not yet been invented, but the fact of sovereignty was there, even if it took a series of phrases to describe it. The idea of external sovereignty was rather easily accepted and there was no great difficulty in defining it. It was obvious that there were a number of political units which were entirely independent of one another, and phrases were soon found which described this independence.

Early in the century, Pope Innocent III spoke of a "king who recognizes no superior in temporal affairs." [1] Later (the exact date and author are still in dispute), someone coined the phrase: *"Rex est imperator in regno suo"* ("The king who has no superior, the king who is emperor in his own realm, is sovereign as far as any outside power goes.") [2]

The idea of internal sovereignty was more difficult to accept and to state in unambiguous terms. Most scholars of the period used the organic analogy: the state is a body; all members must obey the head; all members must work together for the common welfare, and so on. By the middle of the thirteenth century, some writers were saying that this body politic was a *corpus mysticum* (just as was the Church), which would imply that it should be preserved at all costs.[3] This conclusion was quickly drawn; by 1300, it was almost commonplace to say that the head of the state can demand the lives and goods of all other members of the body politic to preserve the common welfare or establish the common defense.[4] One man even argued that an individual should not hesitate to commit a mortal sin if, by doing so, he could save the state. As this example shows, and, as Gaines Post has pointed out, "reason of state" is no invention of the Renaissance; it exists already in the thirteenth century.[5]

But this theory of internal sovereignty came up against other theories of a permanent and unchanging body of law, of imprescriptible rights and privileges held by local lords and autonomous communities, and of irremovable limitations on the power

---

[1] Robert W. Carlyle and A. J. Carlyle, *A History of Medieval Political Theory in the West* (London: Blackwood, 1928), V, 143–148; Gaines Post, "Two Notes on Nationalism: II. Rex Imperator," *Traditio,* IX (1953), 296–320.

[2] *Ibid.,* pp. 304–307, 320. Cf. E. H. Kantorowicz, *The King's Two Bodies* (Princeton: Princeton University Press, 1957), pp. 51, 97.

[3] *Ibid.,* p. 208, but the reference to Vincent of Beauvais should be *Speculum Doctrinale* VII, 15, and not VII, 8.

[4] Joseph R. Strayer, "Defense of the Realm and Royal Power in France," in *Studi in onore di Gino Luzzatto* (Milan: A. Giuffrè, 1949), I, 289–296; Post, "Ratio Publicae Utilitatis, Ratio Status und 'Staatsräson' (1100–1300)," *Die Welt als Geschichte,* XXI (1961), 8–28, 71–99.

[5] *Ibid.* On p. 96 he cites an anonymous author who says adultery is justified if it leads a woman to betray plans that would destroy the community.

of central governments. As a result, the theory was usually stated in comparative terms: the king has *superioritas*, he has "greater power." [6] The theory of internal sovereignty also came up against some hard political facts. Although Western rulers, in general, found it fairly easy to make good their claim to external sovereignty, even against the pope, they did not yet have the authority or the administrative machinery needed to establish fully their claim to internal sovereignty. As a result, there was a long period of floundering, and it was not until the sixteenth century that the more advanced states could really assert sovereignty in all internal affairs. And it was only then that the theory of sovereignty could be purged of some of its ambiguities and stated in clear and definitive terms.

Nevertheless, before this process was complete, another important change had taken place. This was the transfer of basic loyalties from the Church to the secular state, a change which, more than anything else, marks the end of the Middle Ages and the beginning of the modern period. In the period between the Gregorian reform (c. 1075) and the middle of the thirteenth century, the Church had set the standards and goals of European society. When its policies were opposed, the Church had had the support of the bulk of the population, and had often been able to coerce lay rulers by urging their subjects to rebel against them. This tactic was increasingly ineffective after 1250. Habits of obedience to secular governments had been established, and a certain attachment to the laws of the country and the person of its ruler had developed. This was not yet patriotism (except in a few rare cases),[7] but it was a feeling that no outside authority should intervene in the internal affairs of an established political community. People were not very eager to give up their lives and property for any cause, but they were more willing to make these

----

[6] For example, when Philip the Fair was trying to establish his rights over the Gévaudan (held by the bishop of Mende) the argument was over who was *major dominus*, who had *major jurisdictio* or *superioritas*. See A. Maisonobe, *Mémoire relatif au Paréage de 1307* (Mende: Société d'Agriculture, Sciences, et Arts de la Lozère, 1896), pp. 506–507, 517, 531.

[7] Kantorowicz, *op. cit.*, pp. 232–272; Post, "Two Notes on Nationalism . . . ," *op. cit.*

sacrifices for the state than for the Church. It was a rather tepid loyalty, but nothing else was hotter. The test came when Boniface VIII (r. 1294–1303) entered into open conflict with the kings of France and England and found that he had almost no support in either country. Even the clergy told him that they would lose all influence if they were suspected of disloyalty to their kings. From that time on, the only loyalty which had much chance of being built up into a powerful, emotional factor was loyalty to the state or to the ruler who embodied the state.

At about this time (c. 1300), differing patterns began to develop out of the general process of state-building. The most important difference was between the *regnum* which became a single state and the *regnum* which splintered and gave birth to many states. England and France are obvious examples of the first type; Germany and Italy, of the second. Almost as important was the difference between the unitary state with no significant provincial liberties and the "mosaic" state in which a king had slowly extended his authority over one province after another and in which, therefore, each province had had time to develop its own peculiar laws and institutions. England was the best example, and one of the few early ones, of the unitary state; France was the model of the "mosaic" state.

Both these differences are important in the next stage— changing the state into a nation. Where a whole *regnum* became a state, nationalism developed early and naturally, with no great strain or exaggerated emotional appeals. In such a state, people were gradually brought into closer and closer association with each other. The ringwall of the state cut them off, to some extent, from the rest of the world; they were forced to work together and to adapt to each other. They had time to gain a clear sense of identity, to smooth out some of their regional differences, and to become attached to their ruler and the institutions through which he ruled. Where the framework of the state was strong enough and persistent enough, it even created a common nationalism out of very different linguistic and cultural groups. Languedoc was very like Catalonia and very unlike north France, yet it finally became thoroughly French.

It is also clear that the unitary state had an advantage over the "mosaic" state. The central government of a unitary state did not have to worry about provincial privileges, nor did it have to create a huge, and often unpopular, bureaucracy to coordinate and control diverse and quarrelsome local authorities. Local leaders did not have to be looked on with suspicion as men whose primary loyalty was to their province. Instead, they could be used to explain and adapt the government's program to their communities. They gradually began to think in terms of the national interest, because there were no provincial interests to distract their attention. Common laws and common institutions created a greater sense of identity than there was in countries where a man from one province could not understand the governmental procedures of a neighboring province. Thus, England was clearly a nation-state in the fifteenth century, at a time when a French prince (the duke of Burgundy) could still hope to split off provinces from France and combine them with his holdings in the Low Countries to make a new kingdom. The great surge of French nationalism at the end of the eighteenth century coincided with a successful effort to destroy provincial privileges and create a unitary state.

On the other hand, where several states grew up within a splintered *regnum,* the process of building a nation-state was much more difficult. Many of these states were too small to satisfy any political emotion except the desire for law and order. Even the larger ones found it hard to appeal to the same sentiments that were so easily tapped by the governments of France and England. There was no correspondence between the political framework and the ancient traditions of the people. The historical, cultural, and linguistic group to which people felt they belonged was always larger than the state to which they were supposed to give their allegiance. At the same time, many of the splinter-states developed strong administrative and military systems which could not easily be overthrown. Thus, when, in the nineteenth century, nationalism seemed to ensure both political success and psychological satisfaction, violent efforts were still needed to make the state and the nation coincide. The Germans and Italians could assemble and hold together the fragments of their old *regna* only through repeated wars and only by pitching nationalist appeals at a dangerously high emotional level. The Habsburg monarchy was in even worse shape, since it was a "mosaic" state largely made up of splinters of several *regna*. No nationalism could be developed for the state as a whole, and there was considerable confusion as to which nationalisms were appropriate for each of its fragments. The European provinces of the Ottoman Empire were in a somewhat similar condition. The resulting instabilities in these two areas were one of the major causes of the European tragedy of the twentieth century.

Historians look for morals as sociologists do for models; perhaps we can find both in this hastily sketched story. Building a nation-state is a slow and complicated affair, and most of the political entities created in the past fifty years are never going to complete this process. Mere imitation will not solve their problems; institutions and beliefs must take root in native soil, or they will wither. The new states that have the best chance of success are those which correspond fairly closely to old political units; those where the experience of living together for many generations within a continuing political framework has given the people some sense of identity; those where the political unit coincides roughly with a distinct cultural area; and those where there are indigenous institutions and habits of political thinking that can be connected to forms borrowed from outside. Poland and Czechoslovakia are such states, and it is interesting to see how their strong personalities assert themselves even under Communist control.

On the other hand, a state whose boundaries bear no relation to an earlier political unit, whose inhabitants are well aware that their state is only a splinter of an ancient political or cultural grouping, and whose institutions have no connection with the mores of the people is a state which will certainly not become a nation and which will probably soon cease to be a state. Jordan is the best example of this type, though many of the new African states may be as bad. Creating a viable system of states in most of the former colonial areas is going to be a painful process. We can only hope that the rest of the world can avoid being drawn into what promises to be an endless round of coups, conquests, revolutions, and wars.

Nation-Building?

2

Carl J. Friedrich

Professor Strayer has suggested (see above) a number of questions —questions which are not criticisms, but rather extensions of the issues he raised. The first of these questions is: why did such forming of nations occur? What were the peculiar ingredients of Western culture which transformed the initial power struggles, sketched by Strayer, into something much more far-reaching and enduring than political entities usually are? It did not happen in China, India, or Africa, though in all these continent-wide human societies, various kinds of political orders—states—were erected and passed away. In China and India, at least, universal orders were attempted. Indeed, linguistic and other differentiations were more pronounced in India than in Europe, yet nations did not come into being. It is clear that we are confronted here with a most intriguing unsolved problem.

The second question, which I would like, at least, to hint at, springs from the preceding one: are nations really built? Or, rather, do they grow? Even states, the particular kinds of political orders associated with the emergence of nations in the West, may not truly be said to be built in the perspective of many who have considered the question. It was the view of the Renaissance, as epitomized by Machiavelli, that states were built by superior men of heroic stature and that these men deserved the highest praise—at least next after the founders of religions. This heroic view extended into the Baroque age in its classical as well as its anticlassical versions. It was personified in the absolutist rulers of monarchical states who utilized national sentiments for reinforcing their regimes wherever possible, especially in England, France, and Spain.

At this point, the problem of "reason of state" comes into view. It can mean simply those reasons which require rulers and others responsible for states to take the action which the situation calls for, or it may mean, more specifically, to take the technically required action regardless of its possible conflict with moral or other nonpolitical standards. In this latter sense, it sets the lower reasoning of a rationality defined by a purpose above the higher reasoning derived from believed-in principles which transcend the particular situation or purpose. It is in the latter sense that *raison d'état* acquired its particular vogue in the sixteenth century in the sequel to Machiavelli's writings and the practices which they rationalize.

The idea of reason of state had its greatest vogue in the Renaissance and the Baroque period. Professor Strayer sides with Post [1] in holding that such reason of state is "no invention of the Renaissance," but that "it exists already in the thirteenth century." I pointed this out years ago and restated the position recently.[2] None other than the greatest of medieval theologians, Thomas Aquinas, argued that *necessitas non subditur legi*.[3] But,

---

[1] Gaines Post, "Ratio Publicae Utilitatis, Ratio Status und 'Staatsräson' (1100–1300)," *Die Welt als Geschichte*, XXI (1961), 8ff. Here is also acknowledgment of the link, though without recognition of the difference, between medieval government and modern state.

[2] *Constitutional Reason of State* (Providence: Brown University Press, 1957); cf. my Introduction to the *Politica Methodice Digesta of Johannes Althusius* (Cambridge, Mass.: Harvard University Press, 1932).

[3] Thomas Aquinas *Summa theologiae* I–II. Q. 96, a. 6.

although there are definite voices going much further and arguing for the view that the body politic is a *corpus mysticum* possessing its transcendent *ratio status,* they remain dissenters rather than dominant voices. The question remains: why did reason of state become a veritable obsession and a universally acknowledged issue in the sixteenth century? Why does such a vast body of writing spring up in the second half of the sixteenth century, especially in Italy? Is not the *ratio status* different in a religiously and ecclesiastically divided Europe, so that the same term carries distinctly different connotations?

This question is evidently closely connected with the link between state and nation. Strayer implies that there is a necessary link, and yet he also seems to think that there was a state in antiquity. Surely, if there was, it was not a national state. Aristotle certainly juxtaposes the *polis* and the *ethnos;* the *ethnos* is too large for the *polis,* and the *polis* is and must be embedded in an *ethnos.* I prefer not to speak of the *polis* as a state, because of the significantly close link, institutionally and otherwise, between religion and politics: the *polis* is both church and state. In the West, the state, as it emerges, and the nation with it, remains embedded in a universal religion, Christianity. These are all mere hints, but the complexity can be seen in such works as those of Dante. Even while he expounds the medieval order, Dante sings a paean in the vernacular to Italy and presumes a godlike posture by confining his enemies to Hell.

Strayer's view seems to be derived primarily from the histories of England and France, where the battle cry, *"Rex est imperator in regno suo,"* made some sense. But what about Sweden, Denmark, Poland, Bohemia, and Spain, not to mention Italy or Russia? The universal order of empire and church disintegrated differently at the periphery than it did at the center, and in Italy there were no *reges* at all. The kings of Sweden, Denmark, and Bohemia (the last, in fact, usually identical with the emperor) acknowledged the imperial order and hence could not adopt the battle cry. Nor did they proceed against their feudal vassals, as did the kings of England and France. Sweden had operative estates in the seventeenth century. Poland, on the other hand, developed (or should one say, "disintegrated"?) into a feudal aristocracy, the king becoming a shadowlike *primus inter pares*. The development of Spain was also different, since the struggle against the Arab overlords served to generate a passionate national sentiment, even though the nobles, as well as the cities, preserved a large measure of independence until the sixteenth century.

The disruption of cultural unity, which the rise of vernacular languages signalized (if it did not actually precipitate), was a serious blow to the Church and its claims and considerably aided the emergence of the modern state. But the dialectic of this development was such that it also led to the rediscovery of classical Latin. For, once the significance of the vernacular had been fully understood, it was inescapable that the vernacular meaning of Latin, the meaning of Latin in its original setting, should be asked. And this search for the original Roman tradition was bound, it seems to me, to lead to a rediscovery of the kind of political order that the Roman Republic had epitomized. From Marsilius to Machiavelli, this idea became more and more significant, and the sentiment of patriotism was reinforced by the idea of the state. As the nation consolidated itself under its protective order and acquired full cultural depth, this traditional patriotism was transformed into nationalism and as such has molded the political destinies of the West until now.

But in this very period, when the idea of a nation-state has become questionable in the West and its accompanying set of ideas, known as nationalism, has started to erode (partly as a result of their *reductio ad absurdum* by Fascism in its various forms), the same idea has become a world-wide goal of peoples freeing themselves of colonial rule, and nationalism has been transformed into an "ideology" almost total in scope. Ancient orders which were slowly disintegrating under the impact of Western colonial penetration are at present being more or less generally destroyed, and the nation-state is being preached as the panacea for the problems of political order and economic betterment. This means that suddenly the peoples composing vast cultural entities, such as India, on the one hand, and quaint tribal conglomerates, such as the Congo or Nigeria, on the other, are being referred to as nations. No one aware of the realities of politics could possibly maintain that these groups are, morphologically speaking, the same as such Western nations as England, France, and Italy. I used to argue, in confronting the first type of presumed analogue to modern nations, that another term, such as "cultures," should be employed and that we should speak of Indian culturism, rather than Indian nationalism, for the purpose of designating their sense of group self. But political language cannot be thus controlled. The coinage of the *agora,* of the *forum publicum,* imposes itself upon the political analyst and obliges him to adapt his terminology to the emerging political realities and prevailing sentiments. The existence of such an organization as the United Nations, born of the European tradition, but acquiring world-wide significance and being, by that very fact, transformed into something trans-European and, indeed, trans-Western, makes every constituent group legally, ideologically, and emotionally, a "nation." The pride of self of every such "independent" political group is inescapably tied up with the achievement of status which is designated as nationhood.

Does it not follow from this—and this is my next question—that we must broaden our concept of the nation, giving it a more general connotation than it has traditionally had in the European past? It seems to me rather definitely desirable to do so. It would seem that, empirically speaking, in light of present realities, a nation is any cohesive group possessing "independence" within the confines of the international order as provided by the United Nations, which provides a constituency for a government effectively ruling such a group and receiving from that group the acclamation which legitimizes the government as part of the world order. Neither folk tradition, religion, nor any other general basis will do, though these may contribute their ordering share in particular instances. This may appear to be a cumbersome description of a nation, but can any of the traits stipulated

CARL J. FRIEDRICH

in it be omitted without transforming the description into a norm? [4]

If some such description is approximately right, then my last question might be put thus: is not nation-building in the contemporary world something radically different from whatever it was that the kings and rulers Professor Strayer dealt with were doing? Is it not a matter of building group cohesion and group loyalty for purposes of international representation and domestic planning, whatever might be the building stones of the past? Indeed, might not the old nations themselves be such building stones? Are not the men who are unifying (and integrating) Europe engaged in the task of "nation-building" just as much as is Nehru or those who try to weld tribes into nations? [5] Once this idea is clearly understood, is it so very surprising that England and France, those countries in which the nation-state of old was most deeply rooted, should also have the greatest difficulty in overcoming their reluctance to being merged in a more comprehensive group?

[4] Cf. the balanced discussion of the elements of nationhood in Rupert Emerson, *From Empire to Nation* (Cambridge, Mass.: Harvard University Press, 1960), pp. 102ff. He, too, contrasts the "ideal model" of European precedent with present realities, but is, perhaps, more inclined to allow it as a norm. He speaks of it thus: ". . . a single people, traditionally fixed on a well-defined territory, speaking the same language and preferably a language all its own, possessing a distinctive culture, and shaped to a common mold by many generations of shared historical experience." But he prefaces this image by the remark that "no nation ever existed in total purity."

[5] As far as Europe is concerned, it is thus seen by one of its most imaginative and long-time protagonists, Richard Coudenhove-Kalergi. Cf. his *Die Europäische Nation* (Stuttgart: Deutsche Verlagsanstalt, 1953).

The Interlocking
of Nation
and Personality
Structure

3

Hermann Weilenmann[1]

Populations and Peoples

The basis of every nation is its population, recognizable by certain common characteristics, the most important of which is a sense of belonging to some distinct portion of land.

The size of this territory and the manner in which its boundaries are drawn vary from case to case. It may be a continent, an island, an oasis, a country surrounded by mountains, a city and its outskirts, a section of town, a street, or a village settlement. The fact that a man lives or was born in Europe, in France, in Paris, and in that city's fourth *arrondissement* enables him to claim that he *belongs* there, at least for the time being. In this manner, he differentiates himself from all those who do not live in the area— who therefore do not possess this characteristic—and classifies himself accordingly.

[1] Translated by Anna Johanna Gode-von Aesch.

Aside from such geographic classifications, aggregates may also be formed along political lines. People are differentiated by their affiliation with a certain state, a governmental district, or commune, a shadowy image of a kingdom that has long since vanished, a piece of land that has been lost to more powerful hands, and even dreams for a future state. To the extent that their political and geographic differentiations agree, a people has these characteristics in common, thus suggesting a stronger bond.

A further grouping is based on the social relationships existing among people who live in the same area. Portions of the population can be differentiated from others living outside the community through a common *configuration of traits* that forms the basis of a people or a society. Examples of such traits are skin color, heritage, origin, or language, as well as membership in certain political, economic, or cultural organizations or in a particular party, social class, church, or even university. Such distinctions can be so great that those differentiated by them seem to be a separate people. In considerations of this sort, it is unimportant whether the people deliberately selected their place of residence. People separated by linguistic or religious barriers, even if they live in the same slums or palaces, inside or outside a ghetto or reservation, can be more alien to one another than those separated by oceans and high mountains.

This social differentiation may be as sharp as geographic and political differentiation. Just as people can be classified by the color of their skin, so, too, classifications may be made according to its lighter or darker shading. People can be differentiated according to dialects, as well as language; according to sects and dogmas, as well as religion.

By way of contrast, personal affiliations and individual configurations of characteristics related to the body, intellect, or spirit have no bearing on the delimitation of a population. A population comprises all those living within the territory giving the population its name, regardless of their age, sex, vocation, wealth, intelligence, or education.

Of the three types of population, by far the most perfect is the one based not only on affiliation with a geographically and politically circumscribed area, but also on social considerations. In every large territory, however, the inhabitants display such a variety of social, political, economic, and cultural differences that some of them feel closer to persons of similar disposition in other countries and other states than they do to those of dissimilar bent in their own area.

Each person shares innumerable characteristics with innumerable other persons inside and outside each particular aggregate. Nevertheless, none of the many populations to which he might belong at any one time would encompass the total of his own characteristics. For no matter how the boundaries are drawn between people, on both sides there are those who agree and those who disagree, there are individualists and conformists, there are hard workers and sloths. Just as one characteristic does not determine a man's whole character, so a single grouping cannot determine where he should belong for his entire life. The soldiers of two enemy armies, the adherents of opposing parties, the good citizens and the criminals—all these possess more common characteristics than differentiating ones. The tangle of aggregates, complementing and contradicting one another, can be put into some stable order only if the conflicting characteristics, and thus also the aggregates upon which they are based, are valued differently.

Distinguishing Characteristics for Group Formation

Whichever aggregate is foremost at any specific time depends on the given point of view. One can choose the most obvious characteristic, the most important, or that hallowed by tradition; one can give the highest value to the potentially more useful characteristics or those corresponding to ethical, religious, political, military, esthetic, or scientific conceptions.

Who makes the choice is, therefore, of greatest importance—whether it is outsiders or members of the aggregate itself; whether an individual, a minority, or the majority succeeds in convincing, persuading, converting, or forcing the others to accept its evaluation. Not until its general recognition elevates the aggregate to a social reality does it influence the behavior of the individual person.

However theoretical these considerations may appear, they gain a frightening immediacy if we ask such questions as "Are the South Tyrolese Austrian because they speak German or Italian because they settled on the southern slopes of the Alps?" "Should we consider the Greek inhabitants of Cyprus Greeks or Cypriotes?" "Do the Kurds, in spite of their revolts, remain citizens of Iraq, or do they have a right to self-government?" "Is New Guinea a part of Indonesia because it was once ruled jointly with the Dutch East Indies, or should it be turned over to the Papuans?" "Does the independent Congo have to retain the political unity that Belgium had created, or may it break up into a number of tribal regions?"

Any of these answers could be correct. Which prevails in each instance depends upon the strength of the decision-makers' convictions and power. In the above mentioned cases, it depends on whether the United Nations, the United States, the Soviet Union, or the states most immediately concerned prove to be the strongest or whether those who want separation or unification are themselves in a position to choose the particular characteristic that is to determine the group or place to which they belong.

The same uncertainty exists in private life. Countless dramas depict the tragedy of the individual beset by the simultaneous demands of the state, the Church, the community, society, the family, and his own conscience—demands that to him seem irreconcilable. Only someone who feels himself more bound to one of these aggregates than to another and who, therefore, knows which he should give precedence can shape his own destiny, for he then no longer passively accepts the aggregate to which he has been assigned but which he does not like. Rather, by his own decision, he has actively chosen membership in a group to which he feels he belongs.

One such group is a people, and only a population that has become a people can turn itself into a nation.

A Fundamental Test:
External or Autonomous Choice

Whether a social unit is to be considered as a mere aggregate or as a group depends solely on who determines the characteristic according to which people are to be differentiated: outsiders or those who themselves bear this characteristic? From this fundamental distinction the others follow naturally.

Since an aggregate can be set up only according to the objectively determined character and affiliation of the individual, its extent is statistically measurable, even if those assigned to it do not know they have anything in common or if they do not want to. This holds true for a population as well. Its distinguishing characteristic must be recognizable in as many as possible cases and in the easiest way. Since those in the aggregate do not themselves choose the distinguishing characteristic, it is not necessary to gain their consent, nor can they step out of the aggregate as long as they possess the salient characteristic.

The extent of a people, on the other hand, cannot be exactly determined. Before its members can decide in what way they differ from other peoples, they must know that they belong together. This consciousness cannot exist in a people until it belongs not only to the same geographically, politically, or socially circumscribed area, but also until it has the same needs, relationships, and interests with the outside world. Psychic characteristics that lie deep within man are not easily recognizable on the outside, and one cannot assume that all parts of a people possess them at any given time. Even in the case of those who publicly proclaim allegiance to their people, it is uncertain what considerations led them to such a declaration and whether, in referring to the people, they mean the entire people. The only guarantee for belonging together lies in their personal conduct, testifying at least indirectly to their acceptance of the obligations of membership.

HERMANN WEILENMANN

Inner Needs and Environment

The basic common characteristics needed to turn the members of a population into a people are, first, the need to live in their own way and in accord with their own ideas and, second, a common environment.

Needs awaken all physical, intellectual, and spiritual configurations of characteristics and all social affiliation. The needs become apparent when their satisfaction is blocked by outside influences or by internal conflict among drives. Shortage, as well as excess, causes a reaction that is directed at the re-establishment of lost equilibrium, at self-composure, at self-development, and at unification or separation.

Through their needs, men come into conflict with their environment and, if their own needs are self-contradictory, with themselves. Unusual, unwanted, bothersome things cannot be warded off without a struggle, nor can those things that are enticing, desirable, and worthwhile be enjoyed without struggle. Every day man is confronted with these things through nature, other human beings, and the tremendous strength of groups, institutions, and ideas. Anyone unwilling to succumb to his fate without a fight must decide to deal personally with them or refrain from action in any situation facing him. He either defends what he finds good in order to save, improve, and augment it or he tries to decrease or remove the pressure brought to bear on him by changing disturbing conditions or, if that is not possible, by adapting himself to them.

Most people inhabiting the same region, belonging to the same social class, or involved in the same political, economic, or cultural organization need to maintain things as they are and behave like their peers. But their need remains a private one as long as they do not join forces to fight for something they could not accomplish singly. The defense of a country, heritage, state, and all that belongs to them and assimilation into a people can only be expected from those who have this second characteristic in common—contact with a common environment can alone induce them to become part of a supraindividual union.

The individual's personal *environment* encompasses all contact with the reality that he experiences during his lifetime and with which he must come to terms. This environment grows and changes with every new confrontation, new experience, and new insight. His environment is created not from his confrontation with the objects and events themselves—be it with understanding, feeling, action, love, or hate—but only from his images of them. This environment contains what has been and can be proved, as well as misunderstandings, illusions, memories, and dreams of the future. It creates the space and defines the time within which he moves. At the same time it protects him from that which he cannot grasp, from the nameless—in short, from that which is radically alien, although this too, like a flood, can suddenly roar down upon him out of the unknown and unconscious.

The segment of reality experienced by several people from the same vantage point forms their common environment. This, too, links them to one another.

For example, anyone who has contact with the members of a closely knit family, the house in which the family lives and its surroundings, its common relatives, friends, co-workers, and enemies, who shares in some way in the family fortunes and is familiar with the family customs and outlooks learns quickly that he belongs to the others and that they are all dependent upon one another. Similarly, the inhabitants of a city, of a section of a city, or of a specific region can feel so personally and strongly tied to the streets, structures, fellow citizens, civil servants, laws, or history and future plans of their native territory that these become an integral part of their environment and thus the very core of their lives.

Even people who do not inhabit the same territory and do not, therefore, constitute a population can achieve such a mutual bond. For the needs and outside contacts that develop from similarities in race, station in life, language, belief, or some other common link make it possible even for those who live far apart to have an awareness of belonging to one another and, if they are numerous, to dissociate themselves, like a separate people, from the strangers among whom they live. Of decisive importance is whether they have the third and fourth common characteristics that mold a population into a people: an interest in pledging themselves to the common good and the consciousness of belonging together.

Group Interests and
Group Identity

Common *interests* are held by those persons whose needs are no longer directed solely toward the alleviation of shortages or excesses but, rather, toward the acquisition, possession, utilization, care, weakening, removal, or destruction of a particular object in their common environment. Every interest has its own goal: it presupposes that there is a value worth retaining by all concerned or, if it is a negative value, worth resisting by all. Negative, as well as positive, interests can unite or separate people; it depends only on whether the object in question has been removed from the field of individual competition.

Tending toward integration are immaterial values like home, language, belief, attitudes, and the flag, as well as material values such as the grazing lands of nomadic and cattle-raising peoples, which are better used cooperatively than privately; or temples, atomic weapons, and government funds that serve collective purposes from the outset. Unification is also achieved through dangers too large to be overcome by the individual who relies on his own strength. On the other hand, a distintegrative effect is produced by environmental objects that can be claimed and acquired by single persons or special interest groups—a piece of land, a controversial privilege, a position of power—as well as enemy threats and promises that weaken the group's resistance.

Every people has a common interest in defending and preserving its particular qualities, in applying them, and in passing them on to future generations. The greater the love felt by the members of a population for their country, language, and state, the more these values become a common good that binds them to the whole.

Just as the desire to maintain the common good evolves from similar needs and similar relationships with the environment, so it, in turn, is the basis for the fourth characteristic necessary for the creation of a people: the *consciousness of belonging together.* This involves confidence that the other segments of the population will, by reason of their own character and affiliations, also be moved to join the people. But only those who have already discovered that the individual is dependent upon aid given by the whole and that the whole is dependent upon the consent of the individual—can recognize that they belong together by virtue of the characteristics they themselves chose and to which they are prepared to pledge themselves collectively.

The strength of community consciousness in a people depends on how intensely its members feel concern for their common interests and, therefore, also on the intensity of their common needs and relationships to the environment. Only things they value as necessary to life, as important for life, or at least as useful in life will unite them so firmly that they are able to withstand all disturbing influences from the outside and overcome internal dissension.

Common interests grow more intense when they are threatened. Acute danger unifies people more than does the undisputed enjoyment of the things they or their forebears achieved, for otherwise it is inconceivable that those members of a population who pay little attention to the affairs of their country in peacetime would so unflinchingly sacrifice their lives on the field of battle. As soon as the danger is overcome, community consciousness and the intensity of their common interests decrease.

The presence of danger is not the only factor that strengthens or weakens the intensity of interest in the common good and determines the degree of unity in a people. The size of the population and the number of things that its members share can also influence this intensity.

In a small, clearly recognizable group in which everyone knows everyone else, personal relationships are particularly tightly knit, since they include a limited circle of people. The inhabitants of a medieval city or an Alpine valley had more in common than the inhabitants of a large modern state; when they fought for their homeland, no one stayed behind. In this case, though, the disintegrating interests can be just as immediate and engrossing for the individual as the integrating ones. There is no hate more irreconcilable than that between relatives. Nowhere, for instance, were party struggles fiercer than in the free cities of Lombardy. But the greater the expanse of the country, the larger its population, the more extensive the governmental organization, the more complex its economic structure, and the richer its cultural potential, so, too, the more people that may share in the growing number of benefits available to them; but, at the same time, the less able will the individual be to cope with the ramifications of these benefits. In order to make a large population aware of its communal bonds, there must first exist a unified interest that overshadows or includes regional, social, political, and other special interests.

Of no less importance may be the kind and number of things a people possesses in common. A people unified only by the land it inhabits, language, some other characteristic by which it is distinguishable from other peoples, or the state and its organization—such a people seems to be in greater danger of disintegration than one in which the members are bound, like those of a family, by the plurality of its simultaneous territorial, social, economic, and cultural contacts. It is to be expected that people who have many ideas, memories, and hopes in common may still have reason enough to remain together even if their interest in one or another of their common characteristics wanes.

It has become clear, though, that too many communal points may also produce too many dependencies. If everyone feels, thinks, and acts like everyone else, the slightest difference in any sphere of life carries the danger of a division, as shown so frequently in times of revolution. Or the sameness that takes hold of every aspect of a man's life can lead to anonymity, boredom, and conformity on a mass scale—conditions under which dictatorships flourish. As with the mystic, who loses himself in a religious image, or the lover, the artist, the inventor, and the soldier, so, too, a single common possession can be so desirable and irreplaceable to the members of an entire people that life without it no longer seems worth living.

Community consciousness encourages common action. Toward this end, it needs the will to do what is necessary. With the attainment of this fifth communal characteristic, the creation of a people is becoming complete.

The Will of a People

Among those peoples who seem to be an identifiable population because of their particular *configuration of personal traits* and their communal *affiliations,* only some, as a rule, display the same *needs* and *relationships to the environment.* And, of these, only a portion is conscious of its similar *interests* or even its common *identity* as a people. Yet, only those of similar disposition, thinking, and aims can form a true community capable of arriving at unified political decisions and acting collectively. Depending on the goal they set themselves, their common aim manifests itself in three stages: the *will that creates a people, the will that creates a state,* and, in its narrow sense, a *political will.*

The aim of the will that creates a people is to maintain the common good so that it may be uninterruptedly utilized and enjoyed. Not every people with this desire has the will that creates a state as well—the will to create an organization that has the power to protect the common good against attacks from within and without. Political will, in its narrow sense, is achieved completely only by those members of the state who can determine for themselves, from one case to the next, what is to be done and what is to be left undone, so that the purpose of the union will be fulfilled.

The greater the number of persons possessing all nine of the indicated characteristics—that is, the broader the base of common bonds—the more solidly and surely will the state hold together for good or ill. Yet, each of the three dimensions through which the community manifests itself presumes that its members, in their own interest, are prepared to subordinate their particular wills to the common will.

For this reason, we must consider the nature and extent of the process by which a will in a people is created collectively.

Will that Creates a People

The *will that creates a people* is always in agreement with the individual will, but can develop only in persons who want to retain, share, and participate in their homeland, language, state, or whatever else unites them.

The will that the individual has in common with his people accounts only for a part of all the private demands he has on life. Any one of the desires not directed toward the common good can, therefore, obscure and supplant the common will at any time.

Self-centered concerns for the safety of one's private life and property, for pleasure, peace, one's talents, and such social needs as recognition, love, power, or security within a narrow circle of relatives, friends, co-workers, and neighbors—such concerns cannot always be reconciled with the will of the people. As long as the use and enjoyment of everyone's common good mean nothing but the further enrichment of existence and do not touch upon private special interests, there will be no conflict. But if the will of the people encounters a personal interest that contradicts or excludes it, each person must be able to decide for himself which of the two wills is more urgently in need of fulfillment, which of the two goals is more necessary and important.

It is even more difficult to choose when the will of the people meets competition from another collective will. In this case, there is no longer only a private claim opposing a communal one, but, rather, the demands of two groups. The arguments of individualism, separatism, and egoism then no longer count. Both sides are concerned with wishes common to several persons, goals also aimed at by others and pacts in which one is personally involved. There is no moral code directing the individual in any given situation to the correct path: should he be more concerned with the unfolding of his personality, the well-being of his associates, his party, the state, the future of mankind, or his people? A hierarchy of ties cannot be deduced from the number of members in a group alone.

The struggle over groups goes on inside every individual. Anyone who has recognized and decided to which group he has the strongest ties and, therefore, the greatest obligation knows what he must do; but his decision, in each case, depends not only on his evaluation of the common good, but also on the effective power held by the conflicting groups and on the strength of his own character.

For some, the choice is simplified by family tradition and environment. For some, the group to which they will belong throughout life is determined by birth. The vehemence with which a social or political movement can claim absolute acceptance sweeps previously wavering masses along, and many no longer ask what is right and wrong when they do what is prescribed and standard practice. Collective wills function like a magnet that attracts particles. Anyone totally assimilated into a collective organization no longer needs to spend much time wondering how he ought to act at every turn. He entrusts his thinking to the association to which he belongs.

A common will, however, is not created only by insight or voluntary adaptation. It can also be imposed upon men through persuasion, deception, law, or naked force. Economic pressure, social ostracism, police action, or executions have caused many a man to turn away from his group in order to join one which promises greater advantages or, at least, fewer disadvantages. It is less dangerous to submit to public opinion, the orders of a dictatorship, the promises of a dogma, or the interests of those who are more powerful than it is to hold fast to proscribed characteristics, if these characteristics can be changed.

The method of ruling by devaluing a common good, making it despicable, and punishing its practice has been successful throughout the history of the world. The gods and saints of ancient peoples were displaced by conquerors; the freedom of the cities was abolished by the kings; once-thriving languages and kingdoms have fallen; and men, who previously had nothing in common, let stronger wills take over their minds and allowed themselves to be fused into new peoples.

But even in the most adverse circumstances, individuals have struggled for their common beliefs and gathered the like-minded around themselves to oppose the oppressors. Rebellions, uprisings, and revolutions—driving forces of history—grow out of conflicting group interests. No matter how the common will is achieved—be it through personal insight or under pressure—in the last analysis, it is always the individual who decides which aim and group best correspond to his personal desires.

The more freely a man decides where he belongs and what he needs, the more unreservedly he gives himself to the organization and the more strongly he feels himself to be a part of a greater whole. Only the freedom to choose one's group—a freedom encompassing all other freedoms—makes suprapersonal unity a reality.

Will that Creates a State

As long as the will that creates a people remains unchallenged, the members of a people need do no more than enjoy their common good, esteem it highly, never betray it, and carry it unblemished into the future. If the common good is endangered from within or without, however, it is only the *will that creates a state* that can save it.

It can, of course, happen that, without waiting for advice or orders, a people or a part of a people endures tremendous personal hardships in order to fend off disruptive attacks. In countless uprisings, the oppressed have blindly taken up arms against a much larger force, and for centuries persecuted minority families have maintained their language or beliefs with incredible steadfastness. Short of open warfare, people living near a language boundary, in a region with mixed religious faiths, or even those with limited rights under a centralized government need not be told what they must do to preserve their langauge, to strengthen their beliefs, and protect their special autonomy.

But a resistance movement is successful and a collective claim to something can be realized only if the amorphous mass has organized itself tightly enough to overpower the opposing will. A people that tries to protect itself through its own state in this way, however, must not only be determined to fight; it must also accept the limitations—without which the struggle would be fruitless—on personal self-determination. This subordination of any personal will unrelated to the state and the people is the essence of the will that creates a state.

Since the state can only carry out the tasks set before it if every individual directs his energy toward the same goal, it is to the state's greatest advantage that social and personal tensions within the population do not weaken the unity of the people. If the state does not succeed in preserving internal peace, it cannot overcome the external enemy. It is the task of the state to provide the individual with work utilizing his talents for the good of the whole and to help each member of the people to find his appropriate place, where no one will oppress him and he, in turn, will oppress no one.

Like every group, the state must find men who will think, decide, and act for it; it must find eyes to do its seeing and limbs to carry and move it. The implementation of its tasks requires an authority of whose supremacy the masses are so completely convinced that its soldiers will obey it, even unto death.

Even the most primitive state presupposes recognition of the force of its commands, regardless of whether a chief, a king, an aristocracy comprising the privileged families, or all able-bodied men make the necessary decisions in war and in peace. The continuing organization of cooperative life demands a law binding everyone. Every legal, economic, and social institution of the state, its taxes and its police give its imperceptible form a seeming reality, extending to the remotest village and the most distant hut. So that the chain of command will be clear to all, it has always been customary to base the legitimacy of the existing constitution on an ideology rooted deep in history and religious belief.

The state can reach the goals set for it, however, only if it exacts the personal contribution even of those who are not in agreement with those goals. Were the state to leave the decision to accept its orders up to the whim of each individual, it would deliver the population into the hands of anarchy. Therefore, anyone opposing the state's power is punished; anyone not fulfilling his duties loses his rights.

But only those who need the increased power of the state in order to implement demands that are *personally* necessary and important will voluntarily forego the rights that the state must ask its people to renounce. This voluntary renunciation is lacking in those persons who are ruled by the state but excluded from participation in it because their different configuration of characteristics and affiliations do not permit them to share the common good. If they make the necessary sacrifices, it is because they are forced to do so.

In addition to the defense of the common good and the maintenance of internal order, then, another function of the state is to encourage the recalcitrant and apathetic to participate or, at least, not to obstruct. This can come about through the withdrawal of the alien groups or through their assimilation unless an effort is made to protect their special manner of life in the state and by the state.

Territory of a People and Territory of the State

To what extent do a people and a state correspond in any given case? In other words, is the *territory* inhabited by a people at the same time the territory of that people's state?

Since the extent of a state can be established unequivocally through arms and laws (as long as a stronger enemy does not draw the boundaries) and the extent of a people, on the other hand, is open to constant change (on biological grounds, if nothing else), a lasting agreement can be reached only if the size and make-up of the population remain almost the same. The land, not the people, is the constant factor. Economic intensification may well offer room to more people in the same space, but even in this case, the time comes when the unity of people and state can be guaranteed only through the emigration of excess population and the exclusion of foreign immigration.

This balance can be maintained for a long time only in those small regions where boundaries cannot be enlarged and in which a people living together for many generations participates directly in the functioning of the state (e.g., a medieval walled city, a valley surrounded on all sides by mountain ranges, or an island in the middle of the ocean). Since the twelfth century, tiny communal states whose consciousness of the absolute necessity of sticking together gave them the strength to thwart the attacks of far mightier enemies or who were left alone because of their remoteness and poverty, have arisen in many places. Several of them—the Swiss valley and city republics, the Basque provinces in Spain and France, some Italian and German cities—were able to keep their self-evolved social and economic order even after the creation of the great European states. In part, they were even able to achieve sovereignty.

Among the ancient Germanic tribes that settled in the Roman Empire at the time of the great migrations, this agreement of people and state was discernible as long as they held on to their tribal ritual in the midst of the Roman population that they ruled. And yet, intermarriage with the native population and, ultimately, annexation by the Frankish Empire destroyed their original unity. From then until the French Revolution, European history was characterized by two movements: the separation of state and people and the expansion of state territory beyond the region inhabited by the people forming the state.

Feudalism, through which the medieval state in its impotence tried to rule the land completely and establish its authority, soon proved to be a stimulus to the creation of numerous, practically independent, territorial states that, by virtue of the inherited rights of their rulers, remained only loosely bound to the successors of the Frankish Empire. In these kingdoms, duchies, earldoms, and estates, the privileged ruling class divorced itself ever more completely from the rest of the people. They were the noble descendants of the tribe that had originally founded the state or the aristocratic and wealthy whose claim to leadership was based more on possessions than on blood. Over all reigned the ruling family with its court, willing the state and its inhabitants to their descendants much like private property. Similarly, ecclesiastic estates of the bishops and abbots were organized along monarchistic lines. Many of the small states that arose after the twelfth century subsequently followed the example of the large states by leaving the government in the hands of a duke or a strictly limited aristocracy. Thus, the common people almost throughout the whole of Europe were reduced to objects of the state. Any community consciousness that they may still have possessed could now be expressed only by obedience to the ruling powers.

The expansion of state territory took place in much the same way. All European states existing today and dating from the Middle Ages came into being through the annexation of territories previously independent of them. From a central core, they expanded their boundaries outward in all directions, in ever widening circles.

Expansion and Consolidation
of Absolutist States

Integration was undertaken directly by the people only in the rare cases of federation among equals or voluntary union under the protection of a more powerful partner. In almost every other case, it occurred through conquest, forfeit and purchase, or marriage and inheritance on the orders and in the interest of the rulers insofar as they were not satisfied by indirect influence over allies and dependent peoples.

The will of the people was not taken into consideration. The only goals were increased *power for the ruling dynasty,* the extension of strategic boundaries, the conquest of regions that yielded economic rewards and supplemented domestic production, and the acquisition of new taxpayers and soldiers.

The huge territorial states of Western Europe took shape at the close of the Middle Ages. The majority of the people did not oppose this development, for it promised salvation from the anarchy of the extremely brutal fifteenth-century wars and civil wars that threatened to dissolve every type of human organization. But the dukes had to be able to rely on the absolute loyalty of military and administrative overseers spread throughout the country in order to force the feuding families, clans, cities, and provinces to subordinate themselves to their laws. This was the new aristocracy connected to the court by privilege. In its own personal interests, as well as in the interest of the kings, as shown most dramatically in the case of Spain, the new aristocracy suppressed the particularist desires of the urban citizenry and, if need be, the peasants.

The forcible guarantee of internal peace gave the states the power to expand their sphere of influence even further. In Great Britain, the kings of England extended their realm throughout the isles in the wars against the Anglo-Saxons, Welsh, Scots, Irish, and their own aristocracy. For centuries they held half of France in their possession, and they gained a foothold in North America and, shortly thereafter, in India and Africa as well. Starting from the Île de France, France was extended south and west and to Normandy, Burgundy, Brittany, Corsica, Lorraine, and Alsace, which were joined to it; there were forays into Italy, the Orient, and America; in this way Provencal-, Celtic-, Basque-, Italian-, and German-speaking peoples became Frenchmen. In Spain, old Castile annexed the northwestern kingdoms of the Iberian peninsula, the Basque provinces, the Moorish south, Aragon, Catalonia (which had conquered Sardinia, southern Italy, and parts of Greece), Navarre, areas along the African seacoast, and South and Latin America up to California. The Habsburgs expanded their rule from Austria eastward and southward over Czechs, Slovaks, Ukrainians, Hungarians, Poles, Italians, Slovenes, Croats, Serbs, and Jews. Moscow became the center of an empire extending from Prussia all the way to the Pacific Ocean and, at times, Alaska, and encompassing innumerable peoples of differing languages and faiths, thus linking Europe with Asia.

Although the expansionist drive of the kings often seemed totally irrational, it was based, consciously or unconsciously, on the idea of a territory simultaneously defining the extent of the state and the people.

The sea formed the natural boundary for Great Britain. France—surrounded on three sides by the sea and separated from Spain, Italy, and Switzerland by mountains, and from southern Germany by the Rhine—has only one boundary (between Alsace and the North Sea) not marked by nature. Spain is separated from the rest of Europe by the Pyrenees, as is Italy by the Alps. Germany, too, extends from the Alps to the sea; but, because it does not have a natural boundary on either the west or the east, it is constantly tempted to draw artificial boundaries corresponding to its power at any given time.

The readiness of states to recognize mountains and bodies of water as the limits of their domain vouches for their willingness, at least in these places, to get along with each other. Only rarely are mountains so impassable that they could really prevent an enemy attack; rivers unite as well as separate. Even across oceans, people have remained conscious of their belonging together for long periods of time. Moreover, mountains appear as a dividing wall only when seen from the plains. For the people living in them, the way of life on either slope is so similar and the traffic through the passes binds the economies so closely that "pass states" established themselves here and there, extending from one end of the mountains to the other.[2] Nevertheless the lowland powers tore Navarre asunder along the watershed in the sixteenth century and did the same to Dauphiné and Savoy in the eighteenth and to the Tyrol in the twentieth. Only

---

[2] The term "pass state" has been used to designate a state located astride a mountain pass and drawing economic sustenance from traffic flowing through the pass. Switzerland, Dauphiné, Savoy, and Tyrol were all pass states of this kind. See Albrecht Haushofer, *Pass-staten in den Alpen* (Berlin: K. Vowinckel, 1928).

Switzerland, astride the Alps and wedged between Italy and Germany, continues to perform a unifying function.

Wherever they could not draw geographic boundaries for the continental states, men turned to historical arguments. Italians and Spaniards knew that their two countries had received their names and become political entities in Roman times. France clung to Caesar's assertion that the Rhine created a boundary for Gaul, although German has been spoken on both sides of the river ever since. On the other hand, in the German duchies, it was never forgotten that the Holy Roman Empire had at one time united all of Central Europe and parts of Italy and France. Since the boundaries with which the French sought to justify their claim to German territory and with which the Germans sought to justify their claims to French territory were from twenty to sixty miles apart, weapons decided which was the correct one.

Since only the ruling class had to have the will that creates a state and the inhabitants were not consulted about whom they were to obey, little attention was paid to the character and affiliations of the people in the states formed after the fifteenth century. The government's power was not affected by differences in language, customs, local institutions, or regional associations. Therefore, it was not necessary to weld the subjects into a single whole. Even absolutism permitted traditional patterns of life to continue in particular districts as long as they did not contradict the *raison d'état*. Faith alone had to be uniform throughout the state, a fact that gave rise to grisly civil wars, deportations, and exterminations almost everywhere.

The age of Enlightenment loosened the rigidity of the existing structures. The larger the number of people who learned to read and write, the greater the expansion of communication media, the greater the intellectuals' concern with matters of state, the more widely people realized the inability of their governments to solve pressing social, economic, and political problems. In time, clerics, lawyers, doctors, and artists rose from the middle class and rural strata to break through the traditional class barriers. They shattered the firm belief that the highborn were of better human quality, if only by the fact that they were able to conduct more interesting conversations in the salons of the great world than were the proud aristocrats and their lackeys.

It was in France that the power of the state had originally, and in its most pompous form, been concentrated in the person of the king, leading to near deification. And, only a few years after the confederation of the North American states, it was in France that the idea of divine right first collapsed.

Political Will
and Revolt of the People

The French Revolution, by removing the king from the throne, executing him, and suspending the privileges of the nobility and the clerics, annihilated those who had borne the unity of the state and had been the sole possessors of sovereignty. Those who had formerly been suppressed had to assume not only the will that creates a people and a state, but also the *political will* in its narrower sense.

To guide the state—now without a head—safely through the dangerous period to a better future, France needed a new authority. The new authority had to be capable of filling the vacancies brought about by the elimination of the court, church, and nobility; it had to make decisions about war and peace and provide for legislation, administration, and jurisdiction; it had to reform the economy and create a social order based on equality; and it had to be strong enough to carry out the revolution against all odds.

The intellectual leaders of the revolution could have replaced the former rulers with a new dynasty or the nobility with another privileged class; they could have handed the executive power to a particular social group, the provinces, the cities, the administrators, or the army. But they did not wish to rest satisfied with a mere transfer of power. By declaring all individuals comprising the French people to be the sovereign, they changed the course of world history.

Their grandiose theory did, of course, prove to be impracticable. For centuries under the monarchy, the people had not been able to cultivate a community consciousness, and there was no time to compensate for this long-standing neglect. The separation of classes, lack of education, differing ways of life in the various sections of the country, total inexperience in affairs of state, and insufficient understanding of the goals of the revolution itself all made more difficult the formation of a will that creates a people and a state. Moreover, the population, still in the process of becoming a people, could not yet be expected to have the political will that would have enabled it to be the successor of the kings.

It is true that the hope that the healing powers of the promised *liberté, égalité,* and *fraternité* could purify the people like a flame or unite them into a community was not fulfilled. But, even so, they did not lack the characteristics that made the French recognizable as a distinct population. Their sense of belonging to a territory, naturally and historically long established as French, separated them from other peoples. The great majority of the inhabitants spoke or understood French, and most of them had accepted the manner of living and thinking that had long been cultivated in the country. But a third common characteristic was necessary for the political guidance of a unified and indivisible French republic: a steadfast revolutionary conviction, instilled only in the members of the third estate.

As long as the French people, thus defined, were incapable of taking over the government, ever smaller revolutionary parties ruled in their name, attaining absolute power through the extermination of their opponents. Only the wars that France had to wage against the reactionary powers of Europe made the French conscious of the fact that common interests united them into a people and that the state that they defended was their own state. Since then, common attachment to the land, to a people recognizable by its language, and to one's own state have become, almost everywhere, the hallmark of nations.

Nation-Building
in America:
The Colonial Years

4

Richard L. Merritt

The seventeenth-century American colonies existed in a state of semi-isolation, separated from one another, in many cases, by stretches of uninhabited wilderness and, more generally, by inadequate systems of intercolonial transportation and communication.[1] Contacts with the mother country were often easier to maintain and, perhaps, more fruitful than those with neighboring colonies. To the extent that there was any coordination among separate colonial administrations, it was the result not of the colonists' cooperation, but of the efforts of His Majesty's Government in England. Even as late as the middle of the eighteenth century, the colonists were unable to organize an effective intercolonial defense against marauding Indians on the western

[1] I would like to thank Prof. Karl W. Deutsch and Prof. Edmund S. Morgan of Yale University and Prof. Louis P. Galambos of Rice University for their helpful comments on earlier versions of this chapter; Prof. Leonard W. Labaree of Yale University for many kind favors; and the Carnegie Corporation for its generous support of this project.

frontiers, and some voices expressed fears of armed conflict among certain colonies.

By the early nineteenth century, however, the United States of America comprised an integrated political community. The American people possessed a sense of national community and a set of political structures sufficient to maintain a high degree of mobility as well as a large volume of mutual transactions, to ensure expectations of peaceful relations within the American union, and to enable the achievement or at least the satisfactory pursuit of common national interests. The national government successfully protected those common interests, battling the world's most important maritime power (1812–1815) and resisting attacks upon the national unity by northern secessionists (1815). The American republic was unified by 1820 and, with the voluntary and often enthusiastic support of its population of almost ten million, was master in its own house.[2]

In considering this dramatic change in the fabric of American society, this chapter will concentrate upon nation-building during the colonial years. Three elements of change deserve particular attention. The first is the development of political structures formally amalgamating the colonies. The second is the pattern of informal communication transactions among the colonists. And the third is the growth of common or at least mutually compatible perceptions and attitudes in pre-Revolutionary America.

Functional Amalgamation

In theory, obedience to the Crown and the British Parliament united the colonies politically, while the supervision, after 1696, of the Board of Trade united them administratively. With the passage of time, however, royal and Parliamentary politics reduced the Board's importance as a decision-making body. It remained primarily to investigate and channel colonial problems to the fragmented but authoritative decision-makers and to pro-

---

[2] 1820 was also a milestone—perhaps the first overt manifestation—of a sectional rivalry that was to divide the Union four decades later.

vide a gloss of administrative uniformity to all decisions affecting the colonies. Vetoes by the Crown and colonial control of the purse added to the political decentralization of the New World —a decentralization mitigated by little more than cooperation resulting from royal instructions issued to colonial governors.

This is not to say that there were no efforts to unite the varied political structures of the colonies. King James II's attempt to form a single New England Confederation in the 1680's collapsed with his own deposition; efforts to coordinate strategies in King William's War were similarly unsuccessful; and Benjamin Franklin's plan of union, adopted by the Albany Congress in 1754, met speedy defeat at the hands of both the Crown and the colonial assemblies. The most successful joint effort of this sort was the Stamp Act Congress of 1765; this time, however, representatives of several colonies met together not to plan long-term common policies or to create common political structures, but to raise their voices in a united protest against the Stamp Act.

Throughout the colonial period, there were only two more or less enduring structures performing governmental functions on an intercolonial basis. The first of these was the post office. Although founded as early as 1692, it was not until 1753 (when Benjamin Franklin and his fellow publisher, William Hunter of Virginia, assumed the posts of joint deputy postmasters general for North America) that the colonial post office system became an efficient and effective means of intercolonial communication. The second structure, neither so formal nor so closely coordinated as the post office system, was a network of committees of correspondence that sprang up periodically after 1764. By means of the committees, patriots throughout the colonies sought to maintain contact with one another and keep each other apprised of the latest British maneuvers.[3]

[3] To these might be added a third institution providing a measure of coordination in America—the British Army. This was particularly true during the French and Indian War, when the army centralized commissaries and other departments. For a short period, in fact, a colonist, Philip Schuyler of New York, acted as commissary general. The coordination provided by the army, however, came from London; it did not represent a colonial effort to secure intercolonial cooperation. Indeed, even though British-sponsored,

Together the post office system and the committees of correspondence performed only minor governmental functions. They did not constitute an attempt at over-all amalgamation and at a comprehensive set of institutions and processes to carry on such major tasks as the distribution of power and income, the establishment of principles of legitimacy, the allocation of resources, and the use of force on an intercolonial scale.

Even the First Continental Congress, which met at Carpenter's Hall in Philadelphia, September 5, 1774, was not originally intended to be a permanent structure to legislate for all the colonies. Just as the Stamp Act Congress had met almost nine years earlier to present a united front of opposition to specific Parliamentary measures, so, too, did the delegates of twelve colonies gather in the City of Brotherly Love to coordinate colonial opposition to the so-called Intolerable Acts.

It was this conference, however, that broke the bonds committing the colonies to independent and uncoordinated (if often parallel) courses of action. In lieu of accepting Joseph Galloway's plan of union, which gave coequal control over colonial affairs to the British Parliament and an intercolonial legislature, the First Continental Congress drafted petitions of rights to be sent to the people of Great Britain and to King George III and passed a series of resolutions enjoining colonial merchants to refrain from trade with the mother country. These resolves, termed the "Association" by the delegates, called for committees of inspection in every town or county. Thus, based on a claim to legitimacy that was intercolonial in extent, the Association was in fact an effort to coordinate enforcement functions based on local but parallel activity throughout the continent. The rush of events during the next half year did not give the colonists sufficient time to test fully the effectiveness of their Association in practice, but its psychological significance—the first major breakthrough in the

---

such measures often came to nought in the face of colonial apathy or opposition. Cf., Stanley McCrory Pargellis, *Lord Loudoun in America* (New Haven: Yale University Press, 1933), pp. 67, 102, 184, 354; Edward E. Curtis, *The Organization of the British Army in the American Revolution* (New Haven: Yale University Press, 1926).

formation of amalgamated intercolonial structures—should not be dismissed.

The ensuing months saw the proliferation of structures seeking to perform governmental functions on an intercolonial basis. The Second Continental Congress, which met some three weeks after Major Pitcairn's skirmish with the Minutemen, soon began to assume more than mere consultative powers. On June 15, 1775, two days before the Battle of Bunker Hill, the Congress elected George Washington commander-in-chief of a unified "Continental Army," and a week later it began to issue paper currency. On July 26, Congress established a national post office system, with the venerable Benjamin Franklin as postmaster general. And, before the year was out, not only had Congress created a navy (with only one ship) and a marine corps, but it had also undertaken, through its Committee of Secret Correspondence, to open diplomatic relations with France and other European powers. Thus, during the course of a single year, the net of intercolonial structures, which had been of only marginal importance, had grown much stronger and much more complex; by the end of 1775, these structures were performing a significant number of the wartime and peacetime functions of a national government.

That the degree of integration was not perfect is less important than the fact that an intercolonial form of central government, albeit temporary, had been established. During the first years of the Revolutionary War, the colonies carried on certain functions in a manner not too dissimilar from the operation of a military alliance. To be sure, a Continental Army with a commander-in-chief existed. But George Washington's influence in the decision-making circles of the individual colonies—especially with respect to such matters as recruitment and war financing—seems to have been less than that exerted on alliance partners by the Supreme Allied Commanders in the two world wars of our century, nor did the Continental Congress of 1775 have any more power to lay and collect taxes than does the NATO Council today. In fact, it could be argued that the colonists, in unifying certain governmental structures during the year before the Declaration of Independence, took only the first step along the road that led, by 1791, to over-all amalgamation. But it was an important first step. From both a functional and a psychological point of view, the colonists crossed the threshold of political amalgamation in that year of decision, 1775.

Communications and
Colonial Integration

This brief description of the manner in which links formally binding the colonies to one another developed during the first three-quarters of the eighteenth century touches on one important aspect of nation-building in colonial America. A second aspect comprises informal contacts—commercial, intellectual, and communications ties that expanded rapidly, if by leaps and bounds, among the colonists during these years.

Illustrative of this expansion is the growth of intercolonial trade. The number of ships plying between the ports of New York, Philadelphia, Hampton, and Charleston, on the one hand, and harbors in Great Britain or Ireland, on the other hand, doubled from 1734 to 1772 (increasing from 264 to 556), but the number of ships engaged in the coasting trade quadrupled (from 402 to 1,750) during the same period. Comparable figures for the port of Boston are even more dramatic: the number of ships sailing from Boston to the mother country rose from an average of forty-eight a year in the 1714–1717 period to fifty-nine a year in the four years from 1769 to 1772 (an increase of 23 per cent); the number of coastal vessels jumped from 117 to 451 (an increase of 286 per cent). Of the total annual tonnage shipped from Boston, 19 per cent (3,985 tons) went to Great Britain or Ireland in 1714–1717, whereas 16 per cent (6,171 tons) of the yearly tonnage did so in 1769–1772. The share of the total tonnage shipped each year from Boston to other colonial ports rose from 17 per cent (3,583 tons) in 1714–1717 to 43 per cent (16,766 tons) in 1769–1772.[4] In short, although the shipping facilities of the

---

[4] The remainder went to the Caribbean and other colonies in the New World (58 per cent in 1714–1717 and 38 per cent in 1769–1772) and to Europe

colonies generally expanded during the course of the eighteenth century, coastal shipping grew at a much more rapid rate than did trade with the mother country.

Population expansion accompanied the growing intercolonial commercial ties. From 1700 to 1775, the American population multiplied tenfold. Along with a general movement west, people began to fill in the gaps separating the urban clusters scattered along the Atlantic seaboard. By the middle of the 1770's, according to census data currently available, a fairly continuous line of settlement ran from Penobscot Bay in the north to Savannah in the south.[5]

With the expansion of the population came the construction of post roads, ferries, and other means to facilitate intercolonial travel and communication. This is not to say that the transportation system was complete or ideal, for some of the roads were almost impassable in bad weather. But two facts stand out. First, the roads multiplied and were considerably improved during the eighteenth century. (A good indication of this fact is the amount of time it took to travel between two cities: post office records report that a letter required three days to go from Philadelphia to New York in 1720, but only one day in 1764.[6]) Second, travel between colonies was often faster and cheaper than that between coastal and inland population clusters in the same colony.

Intercolonial mobility made increasingly possible the exchange of ideas among the colonists. Among the many colonial travelers, one of the more notable was the evangelist George Whitefield. From 1738 until his death in 1770, he made seven journeys throughout the colonies, five of them extending from

---

and Africa (6 per cent in 1714–1717 and 3 per cent in 1769–1772). Computed from data given in U.S. Bureau of the Census, *Historical Statistics of the United States, Colonial Times to 1957* ([Series Z 56–75] [Washington, D.C.: U.S. Government Printing Office, 1960]), pp. 759–760. The earlier figure for the port of Hampton is from 1733, rather than 1734.

[5] Stella H. Sutherland, *Population Distribution in Colonial America* (New York: Columbia University Press, 1936).

[6] Seymour Dunbar, *A History of Travel in America* (Indianapolis: The Bobbs-Merrill Company, 1915), I, 177, note 2.

Georgia to New England. The religious revival that he occasioned, termed the "Great Awakening," was perhaps the first mass movement to sweep America. It was the spirit engendered in this movement that helped Whitefield to collect money throughout the colonies (and even in England) for such worthy causes as an orphanage in Georgia, the construction of Dartmouth and Princeton colleges, and the reconstruction of the Harvard College library after a fire in 1764.

Religion provided a number of other opportunities for intercolonial contacts. There was often correspondence, for example, among co-religionists in different colonies. Some church organizations, such as the Baptists, the Friends, and the Methodists, held intercolonial synods to coordinate church policy and doctrine. Although it is true that a few of the larger church organizations were located mainly in particular regions (all but seven of the 668 Congregational churches were in New England, and more than one-half of the Episcopalian churches were in the southern colonies [7]), most churches had local parishes scattered throughout the colonies. To a considerable extent, the diversity of religions in America produced a common norm of religious toleration among Americans—a norm that eventually served to remove the religious question from the political arena. And, during the later colonial years, church organizations contributed to that vital flow of ideas and contacts that created a framework for American nation-building.

Another indication of the expanding facilities of intercolonial communication in eighteenth-century America is the press. The number of newspapers multiplied in the decades between 1735 and 1775. At the time of John Peter Zenger's trial for seditious libel, there were only nine newspapers in all America; by the end of the French and Indian War, their number had more than doubled, and thirty-eight were in existence on the eve of the Revolution. Then, too, the size and news coverage of the

[7] Charles O. Paullin, *Atlas of the Historical Geography of the United States* (Washington, D.C., and New York: Carnegie Institution and American Geographical Society, 1932), p. 50 and Plate 82.

63

RICHARD L. MERRITT

journals kept pace with their numbers: the newspaper of 1775 was generally three or four times as large as that of 1735, and the number of lines in the average journal doubled.

Nor were the colonial newspapers entirely for local consumption. In one of the first issues of his *Virginia Gazette,* William Parks encouraged his readers to place advertisements in his journal, arguing that, "as these Papers will circulate (as speedily as possible) not only all over This, but also the Neighboring Colonies, and will probably be read by some Thousands of people, it is very likely that they may have the desir'd Effect. . . ." [8] Some two dozen years later, also seeking advertising revenue, Hugh Gaine wrote in the masthead of his *New-York Mercury:*

> For the Benefit of those that advertise in this Paper: It may not be amiss to inform them, That it is conveyed to every Town and Country Village in the Provinces of New-Jersey, Connecticut, Rhode-Island and New-York; to all the Capital Places on the Continent of America, from Georgia to Halifax; to every English Island in the West-Indies, and to all the Sea Port Towns and Cities in England, Scotland, Ireland and Holland.[9]

Influenced by the huckstering spirit of colonial times, Parks and Gaine undoubtedly exaggerated somewhat, but nonetheless it is true that many of the colonial newspapers did enjoy wide circulation throughout the colonies and, occasionally, abroad. And, increasingly, the printers found newsworthy items in the affairs of their colonial neighbors: in 1738, about one-fifth of their news was datelined in other colonies, and, by 1768, this proportion had risen to one-quarter.[10]

In many respects, the colonial printer exemplified the growth of an interlocking, national elite. When Samuel Green set up shop

[8] Cited in Lawrence C. Wroth, *The Colonial Printer* (New York: The Grolier Club, 1931), p. 203. The date of the *Virginia Gazette* was October 8, 1736.

[9] *New-York Mercury,* August 2, 1762, p. 1.

[10] The percentage of the news lines reprinted from other colonial newspapers is based upon an analysis of sixteen newspapers for each year, four each from Boston, New York, Philadelphia, and Williamsburg. See footnote 15 below.

in Cambridge in the 1640's not only did he become America's second printer, but he also founded a printing dynasty that endured for five generations and included no less than a score of colonial America's printers in Massachusetts, Connecticut, Maryland, Virginia, and elsewhere. Benjamin Franklin, whose fine hand one sees in practically all aspects of the life and thought of colonial America, was clearly the giant of the American printing profession in the middle of the eighteenth century. In addition to turning his *Pennsylvania Gazette* into one of the more influential colonial newspapers, Franklin manufactured and sold materials for making ink (and even an occasional keg of the fluid itself) to colleagues in other colonies; he collected rags and sold newsprint throughout the colonies; and he lent money to and formed partnerships with his former journeymen (including a couple of nephews) to set up shop in other colonies. Franklin's account books reveal that copies of his almanacs were sold in wholesale lots to merchants and printers from Boston to Charleston, South Carolina, and even in Jamaica.[11] His *Poor Richard's Almanack* was popular enough to warrant special editions for New England and the southern colonies, as well as the regular edition for the middle colonies.[12]

A similar intercolonial elite developed in other professions. Colonial merchants, for example, normally had extensive familial and business connections in several colonies; lawyers, doctors, and men of science often visited or corresponded with their colleagues in other parts of America.[13]

In emphasizing the importance of informal ties among the colonists in eighteenth-century America, I do not mean to suggest

[11] George Simpson Eddy, *Account Books Kept by Benjamin Franklin: Ledger "D," 1739–1747* (New York: Columbia University Press, 1929), *passim.*
[12] Leonard W. Labaree, ed., *The Papers of Benjamin Franklin* (New Haven: Yale University Press, 1959–), III, 262n.
[13] Michael Kraus, *Intercolonial Aspects of American Culture on the Eve of the Revolution, with Special Reference to the Northern Towns* (New York: Columbia University Press, 1928), p. 90; Robert K. Lamb's discussion of interlocking colonial elites in Karl W. Deutsch, *Nationalism and Social Communication: An Inquiry into the Foundations of Nationality* (Cambridge, Mass., and New York: Massachusetts Institute of Technology Press and John Wiley and Sons, 1953), pp. 18–20.

that there were no clashes or divisive factors at work. To the contrary, the path leading toward a dense net of informal transactions of all sorts, toward an informal division of labor on an intercolonial basis, was strewn with many a rocky barrier. Diverse and often unstable colonial currencies, as well as the virtual absence of intercolonial credit facilities, hampered trade and commercial relations. Conflicting territorial claims led to harsh words and, occasionally, even to bloodshed. Religious factionalism and regional jealousies sowed the seeds of mutual antagonism. Perhaps the most dramatic elaboration of such intercolonial hostilities came in a sermon delivered on the eve of the Revolution by the Loyalist Jonathan Boucher of Philadelphia. After describing the New Englanders as "the Goths and Vandals of America," Boucher declaimed: "O 'tis a monstrous and an unnatural coalition; and we should as soon expect to see the greatest contrarieties in Nature to meet in harmony, and the wolf and the lamb to feed together, as Virginians to form a cordial union with the saints of New England." [14]

More to the point, however, is the fact that such a union *was* formed. It may seem truistic to note that the expanding range and strength of intercolonial contacts throughout the eighteenth century indicate something of the extent to which colonists sought such contacts or considered them worthwhile. But—and this is the important point—when the time of decision arrived, mutual interests among the colonists predominated over mutual antagonisms.

Images of an American Community

But what about the colonists themselves during the pre-Revolutionary years? Did they perceive themselves as members of a peculiarly American political community or as a part of a British, or perhaps Anglo-American, community? Were the colo-

---

[14] Jonathan Boucher, *Reminiscences of an American Loyalist*, pp. 132–134, cited in Max Savelle, *Seeds of Liberty: The Genesis of the American Mind* (New York: Alfred A. Knopf, 1948), pp. 563–564.

nies divided by walls of indifference, more interested in their connections with the mother country than in one another's concerns and problems, more interested in local happenings than in events affecting the colonies as a whole?

One way of finding answers to such questions is to examine the focus of attention of one of the more popular and enduring media of colonial communication. It is not unreasonable to expect that the content of a communication medium reflects the interests and tastes of its audience, particularly if its continued publication rests upon popular subscription. Such was the case with the colonial press. The following remarks on colonial perceptions are based upon a tabulation of place-name symbols (such as "the Carolinas," "Warwickshire," or "Livorno") appearing in a fairly substantial sample of newspapers, published in four American urban centers between 1735 and 1775.[15]

The symbols used in the colonial press indicate that, in the years prior to the Revolution, the colonists increasingly substituted self-awareness for their early absorption in European wars and other events outside the Anglo-American political community. Meanwhile, they maintained a fairly steady interest in the mother country. Although symbols of place names located in the British Isles generally occupied about one-fifth of the newspapers' symbol space throughout the forty-one years, their share declined sharply relative to the space given over to American symbols. In the decade from 1735 to 1744, one symbol in three referred to a place name in the Anglo-American community, that is, in Britain or America; in the last colonial decade, the same amount of space was spent on American symbols alone. The years 1774 and 1775 found the colonial printers devoting more than one-half of their total symbol space to news of America.

A more detailed analysis of American symbols in the colonial

[15] The entire contents of four issues a year of the *Massachusetts Gazette* (from 1735 to 1775), the *Boston Gazette, and Country Journal* (1762–1775), the *New-York Weekly Journal* (1735–1751), the *New-York Mercury* (1752–1775), the *Pennsylvania Gazette* (1735–1775), and the *Virginia Gazette* (1736–1775) were systematically analyzed. For further details, see Richard L. Merritt, *Symbols of American Community, 1735–1775* (publication forthcoming).

press,[16] that is, symbols referring to American place names, reveals an interesting and, I believe, significant shift in the intercolonial focus of attention—a shift away from purely local interests to an awareness of events affecting the colonies as a whole, with attention paid by the newspapers to symbols of colonies other than their own remaining essentially unchanged over the long run. Although news of the home colony remained important in each newspaper from 1735 to 1775, it declined in significance relative to intercolonial news. In the decade from 1735 to 1744 about three-eighths of the American symbols pertained to local news, whereas only one-quarter did so in the last pre-Revolutionary decade. The colony that gave itself the greatest amount of attention (an interest shared by the newspapers of other colonies as well) was Massachusetts Bay; in contrast, symbols of Pennsylvania and New York place names were prominent mainly during the years of the French and Indian War, and Virginia was important only in the eyes of Virginians. The saliency of the collective concept in the colonial press remained low, however, until 1763. After that date, symbols referring to the colonies as a single unit comprised about one-quarter of the total number of American symbols in the newspapers.

But increases in mutual attention, however well balanced, do not always result in a heightened sense of community. That America during the 1930's devoted an increasing share of its attention to Nazi Germany is hardly an indication that the two countries were drawing closer together. Indeed, in most respects the opposite was the case. This fact emphasizes the need to consider another facet of the intercolonial pattern of communication —the contexts in which the symbols occurred in the newspapers. Did all or most southerners, for example, look upon New Englanders as "the Goths and Vandals of America?" Were all or most of the references to England in a eulogistic context?

---

[16] In tabulating the distribution of American symbols only, direct place-name symbols ("Virginia" or "Boston") as well as indirect references to such symbols ("this colony" or "this city") were included. In the comparison of the total number of American place-name symbols with the number of British place-name symbols, such indirect symbols were not tabulated.

The fact that few place-name symbols appeared in contexts clearly approving or disapproving the place names represented by the symbols makes it difficult to give final answers to such questions. But a brief test applied to place-name symbols appearing in samples of colonial newspapers for 1738 and 1768 indicates that American symbols appeared in more favorable contexts in 1768 than in 1738, whereas the reverse was true for British symbols.[17] Such a finding accords well with a commonplace discoverable in many studies of American history—the commonplace that, on the whole, the colonies did not grow more hostile toward one another during the decades prior to 1775, particularly in contrast to an emerging sense of alienation from England.

An even better indication of a growing sense of community among the colonists is to be found in their use of self-referent symbols. When did they begin to consider the land they inhabited as "America" rather than as the "British colonies"? When did they begin to think, or at least to speak, of themselves as "Americans" rather than as "His Majesty's subjects"?

Three significant points emerge from an analysis of such self-referent symbols appearing in the colonial press from 1735 to 1775. First, the territorial differentiation of the Anglo-American political community was perceived and made symbolically evident before the distinction between Englishmen and Americans appeared in the newspapers. The predominant image of the 1750's and early 1760's pictured the colonists as Englishmen transplanted in American soil. Second, in both of these changes, British writers

[17] Using the method described by Ithiel de Sola Pool with the collaboration of Harold D. Lasswell, Daniel Lerner, *et al.*, *Symbols of Democracy* ("Hoover Institute Studies" Ser. C, No. 4, [The Hoover Institute and Library on War, Revolution, and Peace, Stanford, Calif.: Stanford University Press, 1952]), p. 14, I subtracted the number of American symbols appearing in unfavorable contexts from the number of such symbols appearing in favorable contexts and divided the remainder by the sum of all American symbols appearing in the sample of newspapers for each year. For American symbols in 1738, the quality of symbol usage was —.013; by 1768 it had gone up to ±.000. I then performed the same test for British symbols used in the two years. The change in the quality of British symbol usage was from +.079 in 1738 to +.004 in 1768. The low scores result primarily from the large number of symbols appearing in neutral contexts.

and journalists (as mirrored in the colonial press) were quicker than were colonists to make the symbolic distinctions. Articles with British datelines in the colonial newspapers identified the colonies as American throughout the years after 1735, and by 1768 they termed the inhabitants of that continent "Americans" more often than "His Majesty's subjects" or even "colonists"; the corresponding shifts in articles of American origin did not take place until, respectively, 1763 and 1773. And, third, these changes in symbolic identification were neither revolutionary nor evolutionary in the strictest sense of the terms. Rather, like other learning situations, they were both gradual and fitful, with a few periods of extremely rapid advances and other periods of more or less mild relapse.

By way of a final note on colonial perceptions and attitudes, it must be added that the newspapers of different colonies followed rather similar patterns in their usage of place-name and self-referent symbols. There were, to be sure, variations, but even these grew smaller as the years went by.

A Case Study of
Integrative Processes

Students of international political communities have found eighteenth-century American history particularly rich in parallels to the modern multistate world. In emphasizing the colonial years, it must be borne in mind that they by no means present a complete picture; the process of nation-building in America continued for years and even decades after the outbreak of the Revolution in 1775. At the very least, however, the evidence provided by the American experience is useful in testing current ideas about nation-building and large-scale political integration on the international level. What, then, are some of the general lessons of the American experience?

First, it seems clear that the growth of a rich community life in the colonies, resting upon common perceptions and experiences as well as a high degree of mutual interaction, was slow, with rapid advances interspersed with years of decline. By the end of the French and Indian War, however, the colonists possessed communication habits and facilities considerably better than those of the seventeenth century or, indeed, of the early 1750's. The politically relevant strata of colonial society had a much wider range of opportunities to learn about events and attitudes that influenced their fellow colonists than had been available before then. And, judging from symbol usage in the colonial press, with these changes in communication habits and facilities came a new set of perceptions and focuses of attention. American events became increasingly more important in the colonists' attention patterns. The idea of referring to the colonies as a single unit was gaining favor. The newspapers began separating the colonies from the mother country through their symbol usage instead of identifying the colonies as a part of a British political community. In short, the trends toward increased American community awareness and an enhanced sense of American community developed slowly, to be sure, but were well under way long before the outbreak of revolution.

Through the lens provided by their changing self-images and attention patterns, the colonists began to perceive new interests that they held in common. Events that may have seemed unimportant in earlier years took on a new aura of significance. The grumbling responses that the Molasses Act and the Iron Bill elicited from the colonists in the 1730's and 1750's were isolated and thus, to a great extent, ineffective. As facilities for and habits of intercolonial communications improved, however, such tones of dissatisfaction could find echoes throughout the continent. An Indian uprising in 1763, less threatening than other attacks upon the colonists during the course of the previous two decades, could become a major topic of discussion in the press. Then, too, the rapidly expanding newspapers could spend a larger amount of space on differences between the perspectives and interests of the colonists and those of the mother country.

The Stamp Act crisis of 1765 presents an interesting case in point. As with similar events in colonial history, judging again from symbol usage in the colonial press, the "crisis" came at a time of important breakthroughs in American self-awareness and

images of American separatism. It neither precipitated nor preceded the beginnings of such trends. It seems less likely that the
crisis itself generated bonds of community awareness among the
colonists than that the rapidly growing ties of communication and
community enabled the colonists to voice the effective opposition
that has come to be called the "Stamp Act crisis"—an event that
then made a further contribution to the developing sense of
American community. Later British policies emphasizing diver-
gent American and British interests met a similar combination of
changing identification and attention patterns in a context of
improved intercolonial communication facilities. And, as in the
case of the Stamp Act crisis, an increasing sensitivity among
the colonists to perceived threats to their rights contributed to the
magnitude of the response triggered by specific British actions.

It is significant that the growing ties of communication and
community preceded any widespread functional amalgamation of
colonial political institutions. Thus, the American experience in
nation-building runs directly counter to the arguments of those
who would form nations, or even world governments, out of
various groups of peoples simply by gathering their leaders at one
table to draft a binding constitution.

In the American experience, gradual processes of integration
—shared focuses of attention, common perceptions of the community and its inhabitants, complementary habits and facilities
of communication and decision-making—had to cross a certain
threshold before such formative events as the Stamp Act and
similar British measures were perceived by the participants in a
common or mutually compatible manner. And both rewarding
mutual transactions and common perceptions of important events
proceeded some distance before common political institutions,
whether limited to minor functions or performing the most important functions of government, became acceptable to or actively
desired by the politically relevant strata of the colonial population.

Nation-Building in Latin America

5

Robert E. Scott

Thinking men constantly seek patterns, and, as in most socially-motivated activities of man, a pattern in the world process of nation-building does appear. Because it reflects such large congeries of people and so wide a range of differing cultures, as well as an almost infinite number of possible distinct historical influences, the pattern varies widely from one culture area or country to another according to the elements affecting nation-building. This paper is, therefore, less a formal study of the process of nation-building in Latin America than a commentary on some of the similarities and differences between the process there and in other parts of the world.

In the global context, Latin America's experience lies somewhere between that of the recently awakened East and that of the West, which has long been nationally oriented. Many European states began their period of nation-building into independent entities and, for the most part, culturally integrated units several centuries ago, but the "new" states of Asia and Africa felt the first stir of nationalism only during the present century while under foreign rule or pressure. In fact, their inhabitants achieved whatever unity they have partly as a consequence of mental and material changes engendered by the modernizing influences or threat of European colonization. Latin America, too, had its colonial era, a long and, in that it transferred the culture of the metropolitan country to the ruling class, a fruitful one. But the Spanish and Portuguese empires were really little more than mirrors of the semifeudal and preindustrial mother countries, so that most of the same social and political factors which have impeded national integration on the Iberian peninsula have operated to delay nation-building during the nearly fifteen decades of independence enjoyed by most of the Latin American republics.

Without repeating what has been comprehensively stated elsewhere,[1] let me suggest that certain imperatives appear to be universal, or nearly so, for effective nation-building in the modern sense. Unless a country can resolve a high proportion of the problems of external relations and internal unity (the latter in terms of both physical and psychological integration), it cannot hope to achieve the kind of constructive nationalism that permits maximum development of its potentialities. The degree to which any single problem or set of problems must be resolved depends to a large extent on the nature of its relation to all the other factors in the formula that produces the modern nation. This does not simply mean that a reasonable amount of progress toward solution of the country's multifold problems must be accomplished, but also that the solutions must be sufficiently congruous and compatible to allow each to reinforce the others. Thus, an inherent pattern of irreconcilable disagreement about social or political values may inhibit development of a strong sense of national identity even in a country with a high level of cultural cohesive-

---

[1] For example, see Karl W. Deutsch, *Nationalism and Social Communication: An Inquiry into the Foundations of Nationality* (Cambridge, Mass., and New York: Massachusetts Institute of Technology Press and John Wiley and Sons, 1953), and *idem*, "Social Mobilization and Political Development," *American Political Science Review*, LV, No. 3 (1961), 493–514.

ness and/or an appreciable degree of economic interdependence. Consider, for example, France in Europe or Argentina in Latin America.

In the case of Latin America, few of the problems of external relations which have historically plagued other parts of the world arose to interfere with national development. Because of the huge land mass involved and the sparse population along the poorly demarcated borders, surprisingly few wars have occurred among the twenty republics, and most of these took place long after independence had been won. In the case of major struggles—the War of the Pacific, the Gran Chaco battles, and the dispute between Peru and Ecuador, for example—the territories involved were potentially rich, but relatively few persons there cared enough (or even were politically aware enough) to dispute the hegemony of the victors. In one case, an entirely new and independent country, Uruguay, rose to act as a buffer between contending rivals.

Similarly, in part because the region is so far removed from the traditional center of political and economic pressures in Europe and in part because of the wall of protection thrown around the entire hemisphere by the Monroe Doctrine, the Latin American countries traditionally have been isolated from the world arena, neither influencing nor being much influenced by international events. A few countries—Spain, the United States, England, France, and, to a lesser extent, Germany—have played a cultural and economic role in Latin American national development, but only the North Americans, among the outsiders, have intervened physically with any degree of success, and this only in a few countries and for limited periods of time.[2]

[2] Some indication of the kinds of events likely to spark a nationalist reaction can be found in the differing attitudes of South American countries toward the United States and Brazil. With the exception of its role in the separation of Panama from Colombia, the influence of the United States has been indirect but continuing, in the form of investment and as a major consumer of primary raw materials and a supplier of manufactured items. Brazil's relations have been more intermittent, but more devastating, as at least eight of her neighbors, who have lost terriory, can attest. Nonetheless, it is *yanqui* imperialism that is suspect, and it is the Baron of Rio Branco who is looked upon as the prototype of a successful Latin American statesman.

Regarding the internal problems of nation-building, the whole range of legalistic difficulties that center around the concept of sovereignty and the struggle for supremacy between Church and state and that are identified with the emergence of the nation in Europe and that still affect some European and even a few Asian countries have had really very little disruptive influence in Latin America, probably because of the historical accident that freed the colonies before these questions became deeply embedded in the politics of the mother countries. Although it is true that during the nineteenth century and even during the early part of the twentieth, the small, politically aware ruling class in a number of countries did not entirely agree on what relationship the Roman Catholic Church should have to the political system (resulting in the development of Conservative and Liberal parties) the existence of effective civil government was never seriously questioned. Forms of government, the balance of national and local power, and the degree of popular participation in politics were all disputed, and the legitimacy of individual regimes was frequently attacked, but the concept of state sovereignty based on the models of North American and European political systems carried over strongly into Latin American political theory.

The Latin American countries have been unable, however, to resolve a second set of internal problems—cultural and psychological—which, from the very beginnings of independence, have set limits on effective nation-building by encouraging chauvinistic nationalism and hindering evolution of a more constructive nationalism. These problems extend beyond the most apparent factors of the clash between indigenous and European culture in some countries or the difficulties of assimilating a lower-class rural population leaning toward traditional patterns into a nationally oriented, more modern life. In fact, they extend far beyond those physical, economic, and cultural problems that Deutsch cites as barriers to successful social mobilization.[3]

This is not to say that the shock of culture conflict; lack of sufficient resources for a reasonable degree of dignity or hope;

[3] See Deutsch, "Social Mobilization and Political Development," *op. cit.*, especially the tables on pp. 507–511.

absence of the common experiences which result from adequate opportunities to communicate, move about easily, and bring the world into focus through reading; and the lack of a sense of competence that accompanies successful performance in complex work situations are not barriers to the development of effective nationalism. They are, of course. But in Latin America, at least, even in the countries where the indicators suggest that developing industrialism and commercial agriculture cause many, perhaps most, of the factors affecting social mobilization to shift rapidly toward conditions which permit national integration, the sense of the nation does not grow apace.

Despite the absence of most of the problems of external relations and of that broad area of internal difficulties which hampered some European states and notwithstanding remarkable material and social advances in several Latin American countries, problems arising out of unresolved social-cultural and psychological questions continue to slow down nation-building. Within this rather specialized field of analysis, the two major and related problems which impede national integration are the problems of identity and congruity.

The problem of identity has two aspects, (1) the lack of any strong sense of personal identity and (2) the absence of a feeling of national identity. Closely related to these is the first aspect of the congruity problem, which results because the socialization process fails to inculcate in all of the citizens a set of dominant values that might provide a basis for consistent attitudes toward the nation. Lacking some such set of common values, citizens relate differently to the political structures; those which some accept, others reject, and vice versa, thereby making it impossible to evolve a congruous relationship between any single cluster of structures and the majority of individuals. This lack of consistent attitudes in turn weakens the citizen's sense of personal adequacy, because he cannot find reinforcement for his own views in a widely accepted set of norms. The other aspect of the congruity problem arises because in the absence of any broadly shared political culture norms there is a total lack of agreement on the function of the formal constitutional agencies. Until the actions

77

engendered by the political culture begin to approximate those required by the governmental structures or until the latter adjusts to some generally accepted set of dominant norms, the energies which might be profitably applied to constructive national development will be expended in nonproductive and often abortive attempts to minimize the effects of political instability.

The empirical evidence on which I base these statements is admittedly rather sketchy. It ranges from my own investigation of the political process in specific countries, supported by reasonably reliable survey research in a few other states to extensive review of the literature of Latin American politics prepared by local and foreign scholars in several disciplines with a wide range of methodological validity. Although my own work has concentrated on a few of the twenty republics—Mexico, Central America, and Peru—my findings there show a pattern, and that pattern appears to be repeated, to a greater or lesser extent, in the general findings of students of other countries. For this reason, I think it may be safe to generalize, always recognizing that the findings may not apply perfectly to any one country.

The identity and congruity factors are important determining variables in the formula of nation-building because their influence seems to remain more nearly constant than do most other, more material factors. The historical experience of the Latin American countries, in regard to the basic social and economic revolutions which appear to be necessary concomitants to the material and mental changes inherent in modern nation-building is extremely varied. Only two—Mexico and Uruguay—have undergone sufficient change to mold most of the norms which directly influence popular attitudes toward the nation into a consistent pattern; in three or four more—Bolivia, Costa Rica, and possibly El Salvador and Venezuela—such change is now under way. In two—Guatemala and Argentina—the "modernizing" revolution began, but was checked by traditional interests, whereas in Peru and Cuba the revolution was sidetracked by the right and left respectively. In the other ten countries of the area, the tides of change are washing at the foundations of tradition, but, as yet, have been unable to shift them markedly. In a few of these, such as Brazil, profound changes in material conditions have produced proportionately less change in the society.[4] Nonetheless, in each of the twenty republics—and this is the significant point—no matter how much or how little the material and cultural factors have shifted, the problems of identity and congruity remain paramount barriers to nation-building. The lag in these areas is too obvious, the inelasticity of adjustment too great in countries like Mexico as well as in those like Paraguay to allow those who would measure nation-building to place great reliance on indexes constructed primarily from such easily quantified factors as proportionate mileage of roads; numbers of radios, schools, and newspapers; or rates of literacy. Helpful as such indicators may be, they simply do not tell the whole story.

Let me offer Mexico as a case study, for two good reasons. First, my own most systematic study of political change and the factors affecting evolving political culture has been made in Mexico. This investigation has been aided not only by the plethora of economic, social, and political studies on Mexico produced during recent years, but also by the availability of new survey research materials measuring the attitudes and values of Mexicans concerning government, politics, and the individual's role in the two.[5] Second, Mexico is an excellent country in which to test my thesis that an appreciable lag exists between the appearance of the quantifiable indicators of nationalism and change —in the attitudes of the citizenry—that presages resolution of the identity crisis and evolution of more congruous political structures.

Of all the countries of Latin America, Mexico probably has made the greatest relative progress. Such countries as Honduras or Paraguay started as low or lower on the scale of material development, but they have not developed very much. Some, such as Argentina or Chile, faced much less difficult physical and social

---

[4] For a discussion of the factors pressing for change in Latin America, see Russell H. Fitzgibbon, "Revolutions: Western Hemisphere," *The South Atlantic Quarterly*, LV, No. 3 (1956), 263–279.

[5] This survey material has been made available to me through the cooperation of Gabriel A. Almond and Sidney Verba, who gathered it for use in a forthcoming study of democracy, *The Civic Culture*.

problems, but they have not succeeded in constructing a truly broadly based nation-state. Mexico, on the other hand, has progressed rapidly and drastically in both the material and cultural sectors during the past two generations and is moving toward national integration. But the uneven rate of change between the material and subjective factors is highly illuminating.

In light of Mexico's fifty years of heroic effort to modernize the country, the experience of the Revolution of 1910 proves that, even under the most positive official impetus, the development of a greater sense of personal and political identity can be agonizingly slow, painful, and uneven. This is true of both the individual's personality structure and that of the polity as a whole, leading to incongruous personal attitudes as well as to dysfunctional patterns of collective action. Focusing more directly on political values, I have found that, despite a clearly defined tendency toward increasing homogeneity of outlook and constructive fusion of traditional with modern political norms, after an enforced legitimacy of over half a century, the integration process is by no means complete in the vast majority of Mexicans, and for a great many it is just beginning.[6] Even among the growing minority of Mexicans who feel positive pride in governmental institutions and the political system that have evolved under the revolutionary regime, a large proportion share with most of the rest of the citizens a sense of alienation from the system in the sense that they do not regard the performance of certain government functions as adequate or they do not accept the legitimacy of specific demands made upon them by the administration.

The greatest part of the population, in fact, has not yet achieved a complete transition from norms producing action patterns appropriate for less developed polities to those required for a modern political system. Most Mexicans continue to think of government in terms of output or administrative functions rather

[6] The data and analytical reasoning on which these statements are based cannot be here included. Part of it is available in my *Mexican Government in Transition* (Urbana, Ill.: the University of Illinois Press, 1959), but the major part must await publication of a forthcoming study of the Mexican political culture.

than input functions by which policy is determined. Not conceiving of themselves as participants in the entire political process, they are, for the most part, consumers rather than producers. Moreover, despite the fact that they express an unusually high degree of self-confidence in their personal political competence and influence, in practice relatively few Mexicans are politically active, and general knowledge of and performance in politics are remarkably poor. This apparently contradictory combination of exaggerated self-evaluation and low performance seems to reflect a sense of personal and political inadequacy with overcompensation in the form of political braggadocio. This results partly from the anxieties of rapid culture change and partly from early socialization experience in family, school, and peer groups, later reinforced by adult experience in and out of politics.

The relationship of the identity problem to the congruity problem is manifest in the difficulties inherent in changing the political culture to one more nearly suitable for a modern polity. Since 1910, and particularly since 1940, when the material factors usually identified with nation-building began to expand rapidly, Mexico's political culture has also altered significantly. In 1910, when the country had approximately thirteen million inhabitants, some 90 per cent of the population was traditional, village-oriented, subsistence agriculturalists or peons who lived on large haciendas and had little or no awareness of the nation or its government. Another 9 per cent of the subjects were aware of what the government might do to or for them in terms of output functions. Less than 1 per cent participated in the national political system and shared, in any appreciable amount, an understanding of, or role in, the policy-making, input process as well as in the output functions. Today, of thirty-five million Mexicans, only about one-quarter are still traditionals; 65 per cent are subjects, and 10 per cent participants, with the proportion of traditionals steadily decreasing and that of subjects and participants increasing (the latter at a markedly slower rate).

The real problem of congruity lies in producing participants. The task of converting traditionals into subjects has been accomplished fairly easily through construction of schools, roads,

ROBERT E. SCOTT

cinemas, and the like and especially through face-to-face contacts
with the more nationally aware portions of the population. The
greatest part of the populace remains subjects, however, and
acculturation almost invariably turns the emerging traditionals
into subjects also, because the patterns inculcated by the socialization at work on both the existing subjects and the changing
traditionals are better suited to this type of political culture. The
feelings of alienation and political apathy engendered in the
dominant political subculture are hardly likely to produce a
pattern of constructive nationalism.

The problem is exacerbated because the political norms
which motivate the majority of Mexicans are highly incongruous
with the formal governmental structures established by the constitution of 1917, modeled on that of the United States. Democratic and representative mechanisms based on division and separation of powers call for a high level of citizen participation that
is not forthcoming in a predominantly subject political culture.
In the case of Mexico, the breakdown of the formal constitutional structures has resulted in the gradual evolution of opera-
tional political structures that can provide the kind of central
authority necessary to govern an uncooperative and nonparticipa-
tory subject-oriented population. These structures include the
Revolutionary Party—the PRI—and the presidency, the latter not
so much in its formal constitutional guise as in its role as a controlling political mechanism. Working together, these two political structures capture almost all the developing interest associations that emerge as the society and economy become more
complex and specialized, turning them into what Pye calls "protective associations" [7] and limiting their possible independent
role in the political process. This is done not only to assure that
the so-called revolutionary clique can dominate the situation, but
also to minimize the dysfunctional and disruptive influence that
undisciplined and "disloyal" groups can exercise on the system.

But the very existence of such centralizing authoritarian
mechanisms slows the evolution of a sense of personal and politi-

[7] Lucian Pye, *Politics, Personality and Nation-Building* (New Haven: Yale
University Press, 1962).

82

cal identity and hampers the development of political institutions on which real nationalism can be constructed. This is the inevitable result of a situation that precludes the give and take of competing interests, with a gradual evolution of compromise based on an ever-widening foundation of shared understandings and values. Mexico's dilemma is that the very mechanisms which keep the society from falling apart do not permit the easy growth of a body of adjusted values which might cement it. As a consequence, with the exception of a very small minority of the citizenry, the nationalism of Mexico continues to be based on the false premises of xenophobia, mistrust, parochialism, and lack of self-assurance on the collective as well as the individual level.

If this situation obtains in Mexico where the indications of change are so clear, where modernization is the watchword of the Revolution, consider the barriers to effective nation-building in other parts of Latin America. In a very real sense, I believe that the lack of modern colonial experience and the absence of really dangerous foreign enemies at the border tend to weaken the tendency toward constructive nation-building in the area. Are not the external threats of invasion and the memories of imperialism the strongest catalysts in encouraging disparate interests to cooperate and integrate within the political process once the material and cultural minima required for internal unity are achieved? It is the lack of this incentive, if nothing else, that sets Latin America apart from much of the rest of the world.

Nation-Building
and
Revolutionary War

6

David A. Wilson [1]

"Building a nation" is a pretty bit of rhetoric, but it leaves a great deal to be desired as a social science concept. The definition of a nation is rather difficult to come by, and the idea of building one is clearly a gross metaphor. A nation is presumably a special form of political community, associated historically and (if properly defined) logically with the institution of the state. In history and by logic, it is opposed to empire. Its principle of cohesion is nationalism—a degree of consciousness of being separate and a high valuation of political autonomy. Nation-building, then, is presumably a metaphoric rubric for the social process or processes by which national consciousness appears in certain groups and which, through a more or less institutionalized social structure, act to attain political autonomy for their society.

[1] Any views expressed in this paper are those of the author. They should not be interpreted as reflecting the views of the RAND Corporation or the official opinion or policy of any of its governmental or private research sponsors.

We can read in history of the dissolution of various great empires—from the Holy Roman, through the Ottoman, to the British—by the process of nation-building. In this reading of history, it is worth while to distinguish the processes by which Western European states made good their autonomy from the process of nation-building. The states of Western Europe first emerged in association with the reformation of Christian authority and the exaggerated development of kingship. The process of nation-building, which occurred subsequent to the establishment of autonomy, is associated with nationalism.

Nationalism in its ideological manifestation is an assertion of a people's right—however distinguished—to determine its political destiny autonomously. It is difficult to analyze this right, just as it is difficult to analyze any right. At bottom, it is merely an assertion of a value to be made good, in this case, by a persuasive political dialectic. Political dialectics are not, for the most part, simply conversations. They are matters of political action by more or less organized groups of people. Political dialectics are dialogues of power.

Nationalism implies democracy in the sense of public participation in politics, since its assertion of basic political right is in the form of self-determination. The sources of power supporting the assertion of this right, if there are any, would presumably be the organization of the populace for political action. The ideal type of this process might be the *levée en masse*.

Karl Deutsch, among others, has drawn attention to a process which he calls social mobilization and which seems to me closely akin to nation-building. An effective national political community must be well up on the scales of social mobilization.

Parenthetically, to me it does not seem necessary that even today a state be based on a nation or held together by nationalism in order to be significantly autonomous. Traditional or coercive cohesion combined with the political competitions of the Cold War provides the condition for political autonomy of elites who, regardless of what nationalist slogans they pronounce, do not base their authority on a nation. There is some question, however, as to how long such a state can be maintained.

85

The way, or ways, in which social mobilization has come about do not seem to be entirely clear. There are certainly a number of distinct historical cases available for study, although the complexity of the total process is a formidable challenge to social science. Each total process comprises a number of sub-processes which, if they can be identified and analyzed, may make the work somewhat more manageable. For example, there are the process of capital formation, the extension of literacy, and the growth of corporate institutions, parties, and the like. It is one such process, broken into its constituent elements, which I would like to discuss at some length: the process of revolutionary war, particularly, but not exclusively, as practiced by certain Communists in Asia. It has been notably successful in China and Vietnam not only in bringing Communist regimes to power, but also in advancing the process of mobilizing the societies of these states toward nationhood.

Revolutionary war, understood as a method of political struggle waged primarily by mobilizing energies latent in a certain kind of society and organized and routinized, can be considered a concrete example of nation-building in process.

Asian revolutionary wars are struggles between conflicting elite groups for control of territory and populations. This kind of struggle, characteristic of our time, can hinge on the mobilization and organization of rural populations. In the prerevolutionary state, these populations are politically immobile and passive. In many respects, the political situation in Thailand can serve as a prototype of this state of affairs. As I have described it elsewhere:

> The stability of Thai society, which is the bedrock of Thai politics, is to be explained by its simple structure of a proportionately enormous agrarian segment and a small ruling segment. These two groups interact in a tenuous manner so that the smaller does not irritate the larger. The character of the relationship between the two must be fully appreciated in order to understand the stability of the arrangement. The rural agrarian segment is separated geographically from the urban ruling segment. The agrarian segment is, in the main, land owning and survives by a quasi-subsistence economy, while the ruling segment is sal-

aried (where its members own property it is usually urban and suburban) and lives on a cash economy. The cash comes from levies on rice exports and transaction taxes on imported goods which fall indirectly on the agarian segment. The agarian segment is uneducated (though not illiterate) and the ruling group is educated. This general social arrangement is permeated by an explanatory ideology based on the principal of differential moral worth manifested in differential status and experience. Thus the society of the Thai is characterized by a gross two-class structure, wherein the classes are physically as well as economically separated, and in which differential status is satisfactorily justified. The effect of this is a paucity of interests in the socio-economic sense which impinge on the political process. The structure of direct relationships between these two classes passes through the district office which is highly formal, and socially (and often geographically) distant. The more intimate economic relationship which transfers goods and services between town and county passes through the structure of Chinese traders. These people, as aliens, are easily contained politically, and at the same time serve the ruling group as a scapegoat for whatever hostilities the market may arouse in the rural segment.[2]

Put in very general terms, the configuration of such societies as they exist in a prerevolutionary state of affairs contains a substantial gap between the urban and rural segments. The existence of the gap along many dimensions of social structure has been widely noted in the literature on underdeveloped societies; it seems to be a result of modernization. This gap, a point of weakness or fragility in the social structures of such societies, is the key to the kind of revolution being discussed here. Note that at some stage modernization appears to weaken social cohesion.

The aspect of the gap I want to emphasize is the characteristic of the rural-agrarian segment which we can call its immobility, or better, its quality of being immobilized. This refers to such subcharacteristics as economic immobility (underemployment), civil immobility (lack of political participation), status

[2] David A. Wilson, *Politics in Thailand* (Ithaca, N.Y.: Cornell University Press, 1962).

DAVID A. WILSON

immobility (caste), and psychic immobility (superstition). In other words, the gap is immobility along scales of a variety of values.

It is into this gap of immobility that the revolution, with its organizing apparatus, breaks. In its ideal development, it mobilizes the immobilized energies of the rural population with a set of organizations and draws them into a great structure of activity. A mere reference to the notorious mass organizations and the endless action meetings of Communist China or Vietnam should be sufficient to demonstrate the reality of this idea.

To the extent that this mobilization succeeds, the revolutionary movement moves that much closer to being impenetrable and irreversible, because the mobilization process uses human energy fully and educates the participants to understand new frames of mind, new beliefs, and new social organizations. A nation is being built.

Carrying out such a mobilization effectively demands resources of leadership with administrative ability. The communication of a charisma or a set of sympathetic symbols has received attention as an effective leadership device to arouse responsiveness in populations of underdeveloped societies. Charisma or similar symbolism is parsimonious in administrative skill and also unstable and difficult to use in accomplishing complex social cooperation. The leaders of Communist revolutions seem well aware of the deficiencies, as well as the strengths, of this mode of leadership. A great deal of effort is directed toward the routinization of a charismatic or symbolic penetration of the masses by building strong organizations. In order to accomplish this task, people of some skill are necessary; it is for this reason as much as any, it seems to me, that the revolution seeks to attract the intelligentsia in these societies. At the same time, it is offering a reconciliation of the gap between at least a part of the modernized elite and their nation.

The tactical use of national fronts, party alliances, and analyses of class interests is directed to the problem of recruiting the intelligentsia. Such devices justify support and participation from privileged classes in activities which are more or less openly aimed at the ostensible elimination of privilege and at the same

88

time explain the division of educated classes into conflicting groups.

It is notable that revolution, to be successful and to be carried through to a state of new stability, must attract the support of a sizable number of educated people. Peasant rebellions in all eras have been notoriously ineffective. But by reconciling the two segments, the changes effected by the process may be stabilized.

Communist revolutionary war in Asia is a highly organized activity, which, in its ideal form, synthesizes military, political, and administrative work. It is this organizational synthesis which makes such wars so significant as a social process. The function of this organization is to carry out a revolution—the annihilation of existing authority and its *replacement* by new authority. Its importance in the success of Communist-led revolutionary wars in Asia is hard to overestimate. The cadre party organization characteristic of the Leninist party is an extremely flexible and defensible organizational structure. It is the most distinctive feature of Communist political activity.

The cadre party is an organization of skills which can serve as the skeletal structure of a complex process of mobilization and action. The skills are various, and new ones may be developed as needed, but in principle these skills are devoted to the objectives of the party as a whole, rather than to the special form of action to which they are applied. The strengths of such a device are particularly notable in the agrarian societies of Asia, with their general paucity of indigenous organizational skills. In this sense, Communist organizational work is a form of technical aid to underdeveloped societies, and as such the party may become a repository of a relatively high proportion of the administrative and organizational skills available in the society as a whole.

More specifically, however, in the conduct of political activity —particularly revolution—the capacity to carry on a great variety of activities in a coordinated manner is extraordinarily valuable. Revolutionary activity demands the capacity to sustain a tempo of development of military, agitational, and administrative work, as well as the defensive capacity to withdraw intact in the face of tactical failure. These capacities are characteristic of the cadre party. Perhaps the outstanding strength of the organization is its capacity to provide leadership for the new energies which become available in a society and thereby mobilize them for the revolution. The party provides the skills that transform a politically anomic and underemployed vitality into political action. In this manner, it is a rationalization of human activity which, insofar as it is successful, *is* the revolution itself.

The aim of the revolution is to annihilate constituted authority and substitute a new authority. The simultaneity of these two aspects of the process may be critical in successful nation-building. The process of annihilation is pursued by such actions as sabotage, terrorism, armed raids, ambushes, and the like which, on one hand, seek to demonstrate the ineffectiveness of constituted authority and, on the other hand, seek to destroy the concept of justice upon which constituted authority stands by such acts as propaganda attacks on land law and other economic relationships, on the honesty and integrity of officials (corruption), on the patriotism of officials (lackeys of imperialism), and on the justice of social relations and social opportunities (class struggle, education and literacy, unemployment, wages, rents).

The concrete conditions which mold the content of revolutionary attacks vary from situation to situation. The revolution is able to adapt pragmatically to these conditions because of its elaborate organization, which places political officers and agitation-propaganda workers in even the smallest groups.

Constituted authority, by virtue of its being established, is largely bound to the conditions being attacked; its flexibility of response has several limitations. The first limit is what might be termed "an inherent obtuseness." Constituted authority finds it very difficult to perceive any aspect of its position as unjust. Yet any system of authority can be explained in terms that make it seem unjust. Second, constituted authority has a variety of geographical and moral positions which it must defend, and therefore many of its resources are occupied in defense against potential attack. Finally, constituted authority, being better supplied and equipped, is likely to have made prior choices about organization, logistics, and tactics which commit it to certain directions to the exclusion of others. The revolution takes advantage of such choices by designing operations to capitalize on weaknesses—for example, the use of highly mobile infantry bands against road-bound motorized troops.

In order for a revolutionary struggle to go forward, it is necessary to disrupt existing structures of authority. It is a striking fact that, in those areas where the revolution has been carried through to a resolution satisfactory to the revolutionaries, the traditional authority was severely disrupted before the revolution got started. In China, of course, a revolutionary process had been going on intermittently from the middle of the nineteenth century, and the dissolution of authority over the bulk of China's population was effected by the invasion by and subsequent defeat of Japan. Consequently, since 1937, much of China was up for grabs among Chinese elites. The involutions of the Chinese Civil War are far beyond this paper, but there is no question that established governmental authority was virtually nonexistent in much of China for years before the defeat of the Kuomintang army by the Red army. Therefore, the revolutionary leadership was not faced with dissolving such authority before it could move ahead to mobilize the population. The situation in Vietnam was similar.

The state of affairs that shaped the development of revolution in Laos is little known in the literature. On the basis of the information that is available, however, it seems reasonable to conclude that there was not much in the way of an effective administrative apparatus to give substance to the authority relationship of the traditional monarchy of Luang Prabang and its government at Vientiane. The kingdom of Laos is an accident of history, and during the years of the French protectorate there seems to have been little effort to modify the traditional way of life. Therefore, the machinations of the various personalities, parties, and political movements probably ought to be understood, at least in their earliest stages, as pure clique politics with little relationship to any social changes. What is involved has been the exercise of traditional loyalties and hostilities. To what extent the instrumentalities of the Pathet Lao movement have adopted the techniques of mobilization characteristic of its Vietnamese and Chinese mentors is a subject worthy of investigation.

In Thailand, the situation is different in a number of ways from the situations in China, Vietnam, or Laos. In Thailand, the problem facing the revolutionaries is one of do-it-yourself disruption of authority and its related social structure. In this respect, the rough analogue for any future revolution in Thailand is more likely to be found in the experience of Cuba and Algeria (or the Philippines and Malaya) rather than in the neighbor societies of former French Indochina. At the same time, the potential for infiltration of critical elements is large in Thailand because of the unsettled state of affairs along the Mekong frontier and the ethnic geography of that area, which finds the same cultures flowing back and forth across the borders.

The difficulties of analyzing the potentials of do-it-yourself disruption are very great, involving the factors of latent conflict related to the organization of authority in the form of civil, police, and military structures. Nevertheless, the possibility cannot be rejected. Terrorism against authority's personnel, combined with other destructive activity (destroying crops, communications, and other property), certainly might increase the general state of insecurity sufficiently to stimulate anxiety and erode the basis of authority—the psychological acceptance of its effectiveness. At the same time, propaganda aimed at symbolizing the government as unjust, corrupt, and alien could match the subversion of the acceptance of authority's effectiveness with a conscious rejection of its justice.

The revolutionary organization is ready to substitute its authority for that annihilated. As soon as the opportunity arises, new governmental institutions at the local, intermediate, and national levels are established. These institutions will produce policies which, initially, should probably be understood as part of the attacks on established authority, since they will suggest to the people the feasibility of alternative social, economic, and political relations. But as the process goes forward, they can constitute an emerging national entity.

Several characteristics of warfare are notable within the context of processes of political change. Warfare in some form is known in almost all cultures. Considered as such, it may be prosecuted in more or less sophisticated forms, but it is a familiar phenomenon. In addition, in all but their most recent manifestations, the techniques of warfare are relatively simple. At the guerrilla level, they remain so; therefore, technologically primitive people can quickly become adept in the use of small arms. Finally, the place of war in the cultural structure of peasant peoples is marginal. It is less likely, particularly in modernizing societies characterized by the gap mentioned above, to be deeply involved in rigid traditional social structures. Warfare might be termed a conceptually familiar and socially flexible activity which can, in practice, move people from one kind of social structure to another through "emergency" measures and practices which ostensibly continue only "for the duration."

The relationship between certain characteristics of underdeveloped agrarian societies and guerrilla warfare techniques common in revolutionary war is quite clear. For example, the existence of widespread peasant agriculture of a quasi-subsistence type makes the logistics of food and other personal needs of guerrilla troops relatively simple. Moreover, the heavy concentration of rural population with characteristic rural underemployment provides a reservoir of manpower from which combatants and service personnel can be recruited. The primitiveness of communications also gives the guerrillas an advantage over organized troop units that may be vastly stronger over-all, but which are mechanized, dependent on more complex logistics, and required to defend the lifelines of urban elements of the society. These characteristics merely permit guerrilla activities to be maintained, however; despite their advantages, it appears highly improbable that guerrillas can do anything decisive to the main elements of an organized military force. Guerrilla warfare, if it is to amount to anything more than banditry, must, therefore, become part of a combined activity.

In *revolutionary war* the guerrilla forces serve a central function. The evidence from both China and Vietnam is that the guerrilla forces serve as the major organizational core for the

DAVID A. WILSON

mobilization of the rural population and their participation in
the revolutionary activity. This mobilization part of the revolution seems to me to be the critically distinguishing feature of
revolutionary war as a mode of political conflict, and the potentialities of mobilization are also peculiarly characteristic of
underdeveloped agrarian societies.

Nation-Building
in Africa

7

Rupert Emerson

I

An old recipe has it that, to make rabbit pie, you must first catch your rabbit. By the same token, to engage in nation-building, you must first find the nation. In the African setting, this is likely to be a more hazardous and uncertain venture than anywhere else.

Nations and nationalism consort uneasily with Africa. During the nineteenth and twentieth centuries, the heyday of the nation-state in Europe, the belief was encouraged that nations are the God-given and easily recognizable units of mankind which will collaborate in a harmonious world order when each has achieved the independent statehood for which it is destined. As nationalism moved from its classic models in Western Europe, the tangled intricacies of eastern Europe and the Balkans and the later ones of Asia and the Middle East demonstrated the size of the gap between theory and reality. It remained for sub-Saharan Africa, however, to expose the full extent to which the shaping of nations is arbitrary and historically conditioned.

Africa has a multiplicity of overlapping and competing political communities, and, as a consequence, its peoples have established no single and compelling political identity. In the national era, the expectation is that an overriding loyalty binds everyone to his nation or nation-state. In these terms, Africa's problem is either that it has no clearly identifiable nations or that they are of such recent origin that they have only a tenuous hold on the popular imagination. The basic political pattern of other continents and regions has been determined primarily by their national make-up, even though the precise frontiers between states, often blurred by the interpenetration of peoples, may be pushed one way or the other as the fortunes of history dictate. The political pattern of Africa is one that was imposed by the imperial powers as they divided Africa among themselves.

North Africa has shaped peoples which have a sense of national identity, and in South Africa the Afrikaners have produced the most intense and coherent nationalism on the continent. In the vast intervening stretches of black Africa, the usual assumption is that each of the new states which has been inherited intact from the colonial regimes is the breeding ground of a new nation, but these states are singularly arbitrary and recent creations which, up to the moment of independence, might have been given a different form and which may still undergo drastic change. Certainly, they were not brought into being because of the cultural homogeneity and traditional unity of the people composing them; each was made up, in very varying degrees, of disparate ethnic groups forced into a single political form by the imperial power. Everywhere in the world, nations have been shaped from diverse and hostile communities which have been brought into a common framework over the centuries, often through living together in a superimposed state. It may be that Africa is, belatedly, in the process of molding nations in the same way that they have been molded elsewhere, or, working with different ingredients at a different time, it may evolve new patterns of its own.[1] Most of

---

[1] Herbert J. Spiro is inclined to the view that "completely novel types of political association may be coming to life in Africa" and that these types "are not likely to resemble either states, or nations, or even federations, in

the continent has stood on its own feet for so brief a time that there is still no conclusive evidence as to which direction it will take.

Although nations may now be emerging south of the Sahara, it seems beyond doubt that such terms as "nationalism" and "nationalist" have, up to this point, been appropriated because they are the favored terms of the day, rather than because actual nations have been involved. The terms have been used to embrace almost every type of African political community and political activity and, notably, include all anticolonialism.[2]

The heart of the matter is the simultaneous existence of at least three major levels of social and political community, an existence which involves not only living side by side, but also strongly and reciprocally influencing one another. The three levels are the traditional societies of the past, the colonial or colonially-derived structures of the present, and the several Pan-African aspirations.

The extended family, the clan, and the tribe are the communities in which Africans have lived their lives and which continue to play a very large role today. It would be absurd to assume that they will not be highly significant factors for a long time even though they are being transformed and perhaps ultimately obliterated by the changes in the social and economic environment and by the political pressures of the colonial governments and newly independent states. Because "tribal" groups drawn from the past have survived under radically changed conditions in Europe and the Americas, it is more plausible to think that tribalism will be a force to be reckoned with in Africa than that it will succumb to the attacks of the nationalists. It is evident, however, that the traditional tribal system is not readily com-

---

the conventional meaning of these words." *Politics in Africa* (Englewood Cliffs, N.J.: Prentice-Hall, 1962), p. 11.

[2] Thomas Hodgkin explicitly uses the term "nationalist" to describe any organization or group, from language group to Pan-Africanism, that asserts the rights, claims, and aspirations of a given African society in opposition to European authority. *Nationalism in Colonial Africa* (London: Methuen, 1956), p. 23. See also Gabriel d'Arboussier, "Le Problème de l'État et de la Nation en Afrique Noire," *Synthèses*, December 1959–January 1960.

97

patible with the new and perhaps incipiently national state structures. The tribes, in almost every instance, are much smaller than the states, and, in many cases, they are divided among two or more states whose frontiers cut across the old Africa. A return to traditional Africa, which may also have an appealing ring to the nationalist, can only be undertaken at the cost of grave risk to the states which are the fruits of colonialism. If, as now seems inconceivable on any large scale, Africa were to revert to its tribal structure, almost every state now in existence would be faced with disintegration, and, in the case of presently divided tribes, such as the Bakongo, Ewe, and Masai, the demand would be for "national reunification" through the establishment of political entities linking pieces of present states.

The tribal system has already undergone serious change in the few decades of European colonial rule. For example, tribes (or nationalities?) which had no common political system or consciousness of common identity, such as the Ibos and Yorubas in Nigeria, have been brought to an awareness of their ethnic and political homogeneity through a variety of external and internal pressures, including the opening of communications and the discovery, by missionaries and others, of unifying elements of language and culture. As Africans in large numbers have been drawn to plantations and mines, and particularly into the cities which have mushroomed all over the continent, they have maintained their ties with the traditional society through tribal associations, which, in the urban setting, not infrequently combine previously distinct ethnic groups. Through these associations, the tribal identity or some variant of it is maintained in the new order, and a two-way flow keeps the city dweller in touch with his country kinsmen at the same time that he is helping to bring the new Western forces and ideas to bear on them. Thus, the towns and cities serve as melting pots for the different tribes and as centers for the diffusion of Western-style modernity, but, even within them, the old ethnic groups have a way of surviving and taking over particular districts as their strongholds, just as the different immigrant nationalities have tended to congregate in their own quarters in American cities.

The role and significance of the tribes obviously vary greatly in different African countries. The one case in which a single tribe—though one with marked subdivisions—embraces an entire state is the Somali Republic, but there the problem is complicated by the fact that the Somalis also inhabit large segments of Ethiopia, Kenya, and French Somaliland, to which the new republic lays claim as a necessary part of the national heritage. In a few other countries that have no such relatively homogeneous national bases, there are dominant tribes which may be seen as the core ethnic groups about which the new nation can form itself—for example, the Wolof in Senegal or the Mende in Sierra Leone. In Nigeria, each of the three regions has a similar tribal base, although each also has a substantial number of minority peoples.

Everywhere, the coming of independence, particularly under democratic auspices, tends to rouse fears of the dominance of one group over another, even though a reasonable degree of peace and quiet had been maintained under the rule of an outside third party. In Africa, such fears have naturally centered in the tribes, which suddenly find themselves threatened by the rule of neighboring tribes on whom they have, perhaps, looked down in the past, but who have made a more rapid advance under colonialism. Thus, the Hausa-Fulani of northern Nigeria held out against the southern peoples' pressure for speedy political advance and climbed on the independence bandwagon only reluctantly and belatedly. The Ashanti of the Gold Coast, confronted by the sweep of the coastal peoples led by Nkrumah toward independence, organized the National Liberation Movement to safeguard a special place for themselves and the northern tribes in the forthcoming Ghana. The lesser tribes in Kenya, where tribalism has recently erupted with particular virulence, have utilized the Kenya African Democratic Union as a means of blocking the "nationally" centralizing moves of the Kikuyu and Luo peoples. In the Congo, the disintegration of the Belgian colony into its tribal components has been a constant threat since independence, and, in neighboring Congo-Brazzaville, tribal conflict has flared in the recent past. The fear that tribalism will take over and further Balkanize the existing states has been one of the major

99

arguments of political leaders against tolerating opposition parties which so frequently rely on tribal support. It has been adroitly said that "every African nation, large or small, federal or unitary, has its Katanga." [3]

The tribes, changing in structure and function as conditions change, are the projection of traditional Africa onto the present scene. The current political system of the continent is that with which it was endowed by the colonial powers. In laying down the geographical limits of the new states, the colonial powers determined the demographic composition of the potential new nations, even though many of the frontiers remained sufficiently porous to allow a considerable seepage of peoples in both directions. Furthermore, the colonial regimes began the process of creating some measure of social coherence among the diverse peoples who found themselves enclosed in the colonial frontiers.

The arbitrary character of the partitioning of Africa can be well illustrated by a comparison of the fate of Nigeria and the former French territories. This is an especially apt comparison because the population of all the French dependencies south of the Sahara is estimated to be about equal to that of Nigeria, although these territories lack the geographical compactness of Nigeria. In the case of Nigeria, which was increasingly divorced from close association with the other British West African colonies by the British, the decision was reached to maintain Nigeria as a single federation rather than to break it up into three or more separate entites, even though it had attained only belated and partial unity. For the two big French federations of West and Equatorial Africa, however, the opposite solution was adopted, and they were broken into twelve parts, each of which has joined the United Nations as a sovereign state. It is possible that certain of the territories involved may have had a distinct enough character to have made continued merger with the rest difficult, although a number of the leaders protested the Balkanization of the federations. For most of the successor states, however, it is beyond question that they might have been divided quite differently, that several different kinds of unions might have survived

[3] Immanuel Wallerstein, *Africa: The Politics of Independence* (New York: Vintage, 1961), p. 88.

at least as well as the individual states (even though the Mali Federation speedily broke up), and that several of the states show few signs of becoming viable political and economic entities. Is it a plausible guess that, with only a minor twist of historical circumstance, three or more nations might have emerged from Nigeria and that the French territories might have yielded, say, two or six nations instead of a dozen? In neither instance is there any firm assurance that the present turn of events will be sustained without further amalgamations or disintegrations.

Given the short duration of their existence and the much shorter period during which they have functioned as effectively organized units, it would be amazing for the colonies-turned-states to be able to achieve a real sense of national identity for a substantial number of their people. Walter Sulzbach has proposed that nations exist only "where the peoples themselves demand the establishment of particular boundaries between sovereign states, whereas other boundaries are 'unnatural.' " [4] It is doubtful that any of the African states can claim to be nations on the basis of this criterion. The "natural" boundaries are those of the tribes or other traditional groupings; the boundaries of the states are alien creations. If the leaders who have taken over in Africa have generally repudiated the idea that these artificial boundaries should be overthrown in order to regain authentically African dimensions, their repudiation has been based not on a conviction that the inherited boundaries are "natural," but on the fear that any move to redraw them might open the floodgates of anarchy, perhaps inviting intra-African imperialisms or re-invoking a tribalism which they want Africa to leave behind. Presumably, they agree with Sylvanus E. Olympio, the late president of Togo, that it is best to work with what they have and accept the new states as they are, "arbitrary and unrealistic as their original boundaries may have been," than to reach out for something better which is presently unattainable. [5]

The next step beyond the level of the present African states

[4] Walter Sulzbach, *Imperialismus und Nationalbewusstsein* (Frankfurt: Europäische Verlagsanstalt, 1959), p. 20.

[5] Sylvanus E. Olympio, "African Problems and the Cold War," *Foreign Affairs*, October 1961, p. 51.

is one or another version of Pan-Africanism, taking that term to cover all the proposals and movements looking toward some form of unity, be it regional or continental in scope. If tribes are already largely outmoded as vehicles for Africa's political life and if the existing states are regarded as Balkanized, artificial entities which have not sunk very deep roots in African loyalties, then the path is open to a belief that the more significant reality is, in its fullness, the unity of all Africans, perhaps even of a great African nation which embraces either the continent as a whole or at least everything south of the Sahara.

This is a belief which is passionately held by some of the African leaders and which none of them can publicly oppose, even though he may have serious private doubts. Its sources and its prospects for success in one or another version have been explored too often to need further examination here. It is defended not only in terms of the mystical conviction that Africans have a distinctive destiny as a single people, but also on the practical ground that unity is essential for survival and economic development in a world which still threatens to divide and exploit. Furthermore, through unity it would be possible to overcome the arbitrariness of colonial frontiers and the partitioning of tribes without risking anarchy or tribalism.

What is important for the present purpose is to recognize how continually and insistently the African peoples are being told that the one acceptable goal, indeed the fulfillment of independence, is the unity of Africa which imperialism disrupted in the past and neocolonialism now seeks to block. Thus, to give only one of its many expressions, Julius Nyerere of Tanganyika found Africans linked by a sense of oneness, derived from a fellowship in suffering: "Africans, all over the continent, without a word being spoken either from one individual to another or from one African country to another, looked at the European, looked at one another, and knew that in relation to the European they were one." And later, contending that African nationalism differed from nationalism in Europe, he warned African youth that "the African national state is an instrument for the unification of Africa, and not for dividing Africa, that African nationalism is meaningless, is dangerous, is anachronistic, if it is not at the same time pan-Africanism." [6]

Over and over again and in many contexts, the identification which Africans make is with Africa and not with their particular countries. *"Négritude"* and the "African Personality" are only two special applications of the general theme, with the former reaching out to include those of African descent overseas. *African* history, *African* culture, *African* socialism, *African* democracy, and the *Africanization* of civil services or business enterprises are, on the whole, more familiar terms of discourse than the corresponding references to the several states. When an African professor of history in the Voltaic Republic attacks distortions of culture, history, geography, and other subjects which colonialism brought with it, it is for an Africanization of education that he pleads, a cultural decolonization which "cannot take place within the framework of micro-nations created by European decisions which, to say the least, were not motivated by Africa's higher interest." [7] In a more political vein, Mamadou Dia, prime minister of Senegal, somewhat unhappily accepts the immediate necessity of starting with the micro-nations, but he has the intention of utilizing them to build "the basis of a great African nationalism and the foundations of a great African nation." [8]

II

Within limits, it makes no great difference, for the purposes of nation-building, whether the units involved are large or small, close to Balkanization or to Pan-Africanism. The limits are those of extreme smallness or largeness. If the micro-nations are re-

[6] Julius Nyerere, "Africa's Place in the World," in *Symposium on Africa* (Wellesley College, 1960), p. 149; "Nationalism and Pan-Africanism," *Forum* (Brussels), September 1961, p. 14. For a general account of Pan-Africanism, see Colin Legum, *Pan-Africanism* (New York: Praeger, 1962).

[7] Joseph Ki-Zerbo, "Education and African Culture," *Présence Africaine*, X, No. 38 (1962), 60–61.

[8] Mamadou Dia, *The African Nations and World Solidarity* (New York: Praeger, 1961), p. 143.

duced to the size of tribes, the problem of homogeneity may be solved, although probably at the cost of viability as a state. At the other extreme, if the whole of the African continent is taken as the base, so vast an area and so many diverse peoples are involved that it is questionable whether national concepts would still apply. In the remainder of this paper, the assumption is made that the "nations" concerned are those framed by the colonies-turned-states which make up the present African state system, but not without recognition of the fact that these states are generally fragile structures exposed to many disturbing pressures of the kinds which have been indicated.

The prime condition for the building of nations is that they have an opportunity to age in the wood, and it is precisely this which the African peoples have been denied. As a purely theoretical matter, it is perhaps conceivable that all the people could be educated to a sense of national identity within a generation or two if, starting from infancy, they are removed from all other influences and if those who are to do the indoctrinating know how to mold the human spirit. In the real world, of course, children grow up subject to all the traditional and local influences of family and the several communities which surround them, of which some may contribute to the national purpose but many run counter to it. Given time, much can be done to bring people to at least the makings of mutual tolerance and a common way of life and outlook. Particularly if they are embraced in a single state, they are likely to develop a common body of law and legal practices and a division of labor which approximates a national economy.

In Africa, these are things for the future rather than of the past. What might be called the core-nationalities which elsewhere have been shaped through centuries of living together are still lacking in Africa except where the state accidentally coincides with a dominant tribe. To give three West African examples: Upper Volta was first fabricated in 1919 and, from 1932 to 1947, was divided among neighboring French territories; in the present Ghana, full legislative and constitutional unification of the Gold Coast Colony and Ashanti took place only in 1946, whereas the northern territories secured representation in the Legislative

Council only in 1950–1951; in the case of Nigeria, the north and south were joined for limited purposes in 1914 but continued to be treated differently in many respects, and it was not until 1947 that the north was represented in the Legislative Council. It takes time to build a national community, and Africa's time has not only been brief but also, under colonial management, only accidentally turned to purposes which promoted nation-building.

A first necessity in African nation-building is to deal in some fashion with the problem of tribalism which threatens almost everywhere to be a disruptive force. Frequently, it seems all the more dangerous to the newly risen national leaders because they represent the new forces and ideas, whereas tribalism's champions are more likely to be spokesmen for the traditional elements in African society. Tribalism has also served to impair the relations between African states where there has been an expulsion of alien tribesmen, as, for example, in the Ivory Coast and Gabon.

At the extremes, tribalism can be dealt with in two fashions —either use of the tribes as the building blocks of the nation or eradication of them as completely as possible, replacing them by a single national solidarity. It is the latter course which is more generally followed. One country which has accepted and built on some of its tribal foundation is Nigeria, presumably less because of any theoretical conviction than because of the size of its population and the strength of the major tribes or nationalities which compose it.[9] On the other side of the continent, the small tribes in Kenya have demanded a loose federal structure in order to preserve their tribal identity—and their lands—in a state which seemed sure to be dominated by the more numerous Kikuyu and Luo and have pointed to the Congo as a warning that an imposed unity will not survive.

It is one of the standard charges against colonialism, particularly where it took the form of indirect rule, that it divided and ruled through backing tribal separatism and playing tribes off against one another at the expense of the national movement.

[9] *The Report of the Commission Appointed to Enquire into the Fears of Minorities and the Means of Allaying Them* (Cmd. 505, 1958) furnishes useful detail on the small tribes in Nigeria which have no direct access to power.

Thus, Nkrumah has accused colonialism of trying to persuade the Africans that they were alien to each other: "It played upon our tribal instincts. It sowed seeds of dissension in order to promote disunity among us." [10] As a counterproposition to this, he said, in 1959 in the tenth anniversary speech to his Convention People's Party, "We must insist that in Ghana, in the higher reaches of our national life, there should be no reference to Fantes, Ashantis, Ewes, Fas, Dagombas, 'strangers,' and so further, but that we should call ourselves Ghanaians—all brothers and sisters, members of the same community—the State of Ghana." [11] It is worthy to note that he makes this plea not to strengthen the Ghanaian nation, but, as he put it, "to cultivate the wider spirit which our objective of Pan-Africanism calls for" by purging people's minds of tribal chauvinism.

A similar attack on tribalism was made, also in 1959, by Sékou Touré, who, citing his desire to make Guinea a viable national entity, asserted—one can only assume, overconfidently, "In three or four years, no one will remember the tribal, ethnic or religious rivalries which, in the recent past, caused so much damage to our country and its populations." [12]

One of the central arguments of those who have created or who support the one-party system in Africa is that, in contrast to the dominant nationalist party, any opposition group is likely to be tribally based and hence divisive in character at a time when building national unity has first priority. In any situation in which the distinction between ethnic groups marks the primary and most evident difference between people, it is inevitable that these groups should seek political expression and be used as built-in constituencies when democratic machinery is introduced, but tribal parties, representing particularist territorial interests,

[10] Kwame Nkrumah, *I Speak of Freedom* (New York: Prager, 1961), p. 212.
[11] Cited by Thomas Hodgkin, *African Political Parties* (Baltimore: Penguin, 1961), p. 158.
[12] Sékou Touré, *Towards Full Re-Africanization* (Paris: Présence Africaine, 1959), p. 34. It should be noted that Touré speaks of "the populations" of Guinea in the plural. Some of the problems involved in superseding tribalism are examined by Leonard W. Doob, "From Tribalism to Nationalism in Africa," *International Affairs*, XVI, No. 2 (1962).

obviously bring many dangers with them. As Selig Harrison has said of India, when party politics is made up of the clash between regions and between regional and national interests, "the political process serves only to drive on rather than to relieve centrifugal forces." [13] In Ghana, where the Ashanti, working through the National Liberation Movement, were a stumbling block on the way to independence, ethnic, regional, and religious parties were later banned by law. The result was the amalgamation of several of the opposition groups into the United Party, which never had much chance, however, in competition with the ruling Convention People's Party. Elsewhere, notably in the ex-French territories, the problem has been met and the position of the *parti unique* preserved by the device of a single national electoral slate with the winner taking all the seats.

The single party finds part of its justification in its "national" scope, but within its framework the leaders cannot help paying close attention to what has been termed "ethnic arithmetic." [14] In its simplest form, this is merely a matter of maintaining a rough correspondence between the ethnic origin of leaders and followers in much the same fashion that a national or local administration in the United States keeps a close eye on the ethnic balance of its members. Tribalism may be deplored, but it cannot be ignored as a social and political fact. If the masses are to be reached, particularly those in the rural areas, the most effective means at hand are the tribal channels. Even where the pre-eminence of the single national party is well established, it will be a long time before it can cease to calculate its political arithmetic in dealing with the ethnic groups which make up the society which it rules.[15]

[13] Selig S. Harrison, *India, The Most Dangerous Decades* (Princeton: Princeton University Press, 1960), p. 308.

[14] Ruth Schachter, "Single-Party Systems in West Africa," *American Political Science Review,* June 1961, p. 301. She adds, "Leaders who tried to build national parties failed when they did not have among their ranks representatives of the most important etnic groups."

[15] A. R. Zolberg has made a revealing study of the tribal element in the dominant party in the Ivory Coast: "Effets de la structure d'un parti politique sur l'intégration nationale," *Cahiers d'études africaines,* No. 3 (1960), 140–149.

The nationalist party may well be the most effective instrument for nation-building in Africa at the present time, although its role and contribution obviously vary from country to country. It is the body which has led the country in the attack upon colonialism, and at its head stand the national leaders—or the central national hero—who symbolize the purpose and achievements of the people. Furthermore, the trend in most African countries has been to consolidate the supremacy of the dominant party not only in the sense of wholly eliminating other parties, but also of explicitly subordinating governmental and administrative machinery to the party. The party organs make the decisions, and the government carries them out; the government is the agent of the party. Nowhere is party supremacy more vigorously asserted than in Ghana, where Nkrumah has said of the CPP: "It is the uniting force that guides and pilots the nation and is the nerve center of the positive struggles for African irredentism. Its supremacy cannot be challenged. The CPP is Ghana, and Ghana is the CPP." [16]

Where well-organized mass parties have been established, a major service which they render is to provide an elaborate communications network on a countrywide basis in a continent notoriously badly equipped with communications facilities. When Nyerere resigned as Prime Minister of Tanganyika shortly after independence but without having lost his status as the outstanding national leader, he announced his intention of devoting himself to the strengthening of the governing party, the Tanganyika African National Union. In particular, he sought to enhance its

---

See also Wallerstein, "Ethnicity and National Integration in West Africa, pp. 129–139" in the same issue and Richard L. Sklar, "The Contribution of Tribalism to Nationalism in Western Nigeria," *Journal of Human Relations*, VIII, Nos. 3–4 (1960), 407–418.

[16] Nkrumah, *op. cit.*, p. 209. Sékou Touré similarly sees his Democratic Party as representing the people, the nation, and the destiny of Guinea: "De ce fait, notre Parti ne doit-il pas, dans tous les secteurs actifs de la vie guinéenne exiger le respect de sa ligne politique, appliquer sa dictature qui est une dictature démocratique, puisque ses principes sont definis en Congrès et en assemblées, une dictature populaire, puisque son contenu ne tend qu'à sauvegarder et à développer la liberté et les droits du peuple." *La Guinée et l'émancipation africaine*, (Paris: Présence Africaine, 1959), p. 217.

role as a two-way street leading from the center of the country to every outlying village and from the villages to the center. The creation by the parties of provincial and local branches or cells means that people throughout the country are being drawn into some measure of contact with the national political life. Whether or not it is overtly so labeled, the principle of democratic central-ism is assumed to exist and to have opened all issues to public discussion until final decisions are reached. Even where, as is very widely the case, the electorate is presented with only a single candidate or list to vote on, the fact that the suffrage is universal and that election campaigns are carried on has an educational impact and, presumably, conveys some sense of popular participa-tion, and stimulates political awareness. In addition to its own immediate organizational structure, the party is also likely to use, and perhaps to draw directly into its ambit, a variety of other organizations for such special groups as laborers, farmers, women, and youth, creating a nationally centered network which reaches to every corner of the country and envisages the mobilization of every group. In this connection, the ability to hold the trade unions in line as agents of the party is particularly important, and the organizing experience and public prestige which trade union leaders have secured has not infrequently been turned to political advantage.

In the old established nations of other parts of the world, it is reasonable to assume wide areas of consensus in political and social spheres, whereas in Africa, the disparities between different elements of the society are so great that any such as-sumption is illusory. In a somewhat different sense from that in which J.S. Furnivall originally used the term, the African coun-tries tend to be plural societies marked by the absence of any identifiable and coherent social will. For them (as perhaps for all others as well) the easiest means of securing a united popular front is to point to the alien enemy, the hostile "they" who threaten the security and well-being of the friendly and familiar "we," even though the "we" has been unaware of its common identity up to this point. In the colonial situation, it is the nationalist party which represents the incipient nation against the

alien rulers and hence becomes the flame to ignite the consciousness of national community.

"Most African nations do not have long histories as nationalities," Immanuel Wallerstein has written. "Their nationhood has
been created in the crucible of a revolutionary struggle against
a colonial power. The unity of the nation was forged in the fight
against the external enemy." [17] The experience of joining in com-
bat against the imperial forces is undoubtedly a major element
in nation-building, but for many, indeed for most, of the African
countries, the revolutionary struggle is not only of very recent
origin but also has never been fought at a very high pitch.
Colonialism was certainly detested, particularly by those who had
close contact with the West, and the anticolonial movement was
in one stage or another of preparation or action everywhere.
But the African nationalist pot was just beginning to boil over
in the 1950's, when Britain and France, later hastily joined by
Belgium, were already concluding that colonial warfare was no
longer worth fighting. Only where white settlers in substantial
numbers were involved, as in Algeria and, in decreasing degree,
in the Rhodesias and Kenya, was significant resistance offered
to the nationalist movements after the general climate of opinion
in the imperial centers and in the world at large had swung
against the continued maintenance of empire. The Mau Mau
uprising was met with bitter resistance, but it came a little early
and it also represented a tribal xenophobia rather than a modern
national movement; and, if de Gaulle took revenge on Guinea for
its "no" vote in the 1958 plebiscite, he speedily turned to acceptance of the demand for independence of the other French African
territories.[18] On this ground, it has been argued that most of the
Africans have been cheated of their revolution and that some of

[17] Wallerstein, *op. cit.*, p. 85.
[18] David Williams has commented on the "really extraordinary phenomenon" of the ex-French colonies', including Guinea and Mali, achieving
independence without any campaign of the kind engaged in by Ghana. "For
them, independence has never been a popular political issue so much as a
matter for negotiation between African and French leaders. In Ghana there
was nationalism without a nation; in the ex-French territories they have to
build nations without nationalism." "How Deep the Split in West Africa?"
Foreign Affairs, October 1961, p. 125.

them feel that independence so easily won is neither real nor trustworthy. The forging of national unity required a more vehement revolution and a sterner resistance than the bulk of the African countries actually experienced. In some instances, one has a sense of witnessing the creation of a myth which no doubt serves useful social and psychological purposes in reading of the heroic struggle for independence waged by the nationalists; actually, however, the available evidence suggests that, once the anticolonial drive picked up momentum, there was a large measure of collaboration between the nationalists and the colonial authorities in preparation for the forthcoming turnover of power.

When independence is won, the plea for national unity in the face of the external enemy becomes more difficult to maintain, and the internal cleavages which may have been temporarily subordinated to the united front are likely to assert themselves. At this point, the demand for a one-party system has often been vigorously put forward not only to safeguard the power of those who have succeeded the colonial regime, but also to build the nation, consolidate the state structure, and speed economic and social development. It would be difficult to challenge the argument that the crisis which confronts the new countries is quite as urgent as that surrounding the struggle for freedom. In the quest for unity, the recently elaborated doctrine of the threat of neocolonialism—the alleged effort of the imperialists to stay in control by more subtle means, particularly through economic domination—is utilized to demonstrate that vigilance cannot safely be relaxed and that the old enemy is as much a menace as ever.

For the rest, the ideas and the machineries which Africans can draw upon for their nation-building differ from those available in other parts of the world only in those aspects in which Africa itself differs. When balanced, these differences tend to tell against an easy transition into the national era for Africa.

One obvious channel for national indoctrination is the apparatus for formal education, the entire school system. Although the newly independent countries are rapidly expanding their educational systems, illiteracy still remains the rule rather than the exception, and inevitably it will be some time before an effective general literacy is achieved. The available evidence is scanty, but it is improbable that the educational authorities have thus far made any significant direct effort to use the schools as agencies for "nationalizing" the pupils. The missionary and colonial origins of the schools, which precluded nationalist indoctrination, have continued into the period of independence, and the teaching materials and concepts necessary for nationalistic indoctrination are not yet available. In the first phase, attention is concentrated on providing the bare necessities—schools, teachers, and materials —although the local production of textbooks is often under way and new "national" histories are being prepared. The mere fact that more and more children are securing at least the rudiments of education in a national school system must have an important effect in producing the like-mindedness which is the foundation of a nation, but to move beyond this into deliberate indoctrination presumably requires more academic abundance and political and academic sophistication.

A major element in building a sense of identification with the nation is the belief in a common and distinguished history and tradition. Everywhere as much myth as reality enters this process, but the recent and arbitrary character of the African state system renders it especially difficult to find a past for the emergent African nations. The distinguished Nigerian historian K. Onwuka Dike has rightly contended that such seemingly abstract considerations as history and culture are as important as more material ones in nation-building. In his opinion, African self-government cannot succeed if the African has no heritage and no future except as an imitation European.

> But if the instinctive belief of the African in his traditions is justified, the ultimate emergence of West African states as independent modern nations cannot be doubted. . . . Every nation builds its future on its past; so the African must not only instinctively have faith in his own existence, but must also satisfy himself by scientific inquiry that it exists.[19]

[19] K. Onwuka Dike, "History and African Nationalism," *Proceedings of the First Annual Conference of the West African Institute of Social and Economic Research* (Ibadan: University College, 1952. Reprinted 1957), p. 31.

Much has been done in recent years to rehabilitate African history and to restore African tradition to a place of honor, but the descriptive word is "African" and not the name of any one African country. To go back further than the brief colonial period is to inescapably come upon the tribes and their relations, hostile or friendly, with one another. The alternative is to abstract from the concrete reality a picture of the great African continent in its totality. Here, as in so many other respects, Africa differs from other parts of the world only in that its transition to nationhood comes so late.

It was central to the European experience and that of some other peoples that language and nation had a large measure of coincidence. Although exceptions immediately come to mind, it was assumed that those who spoke Italian were Italians and those who spoke French were Frenchmen. As nationalism has spread around the globe, the identification of the nation with the linguistic community has become an increasingly dubious proposition, although it inevitably remains the fact that those who speak the same language have a social bond of inestimable value. In a number of new countries, the ability of the people to communicate with one another is circumscribed by the diversity of their mother tongues. Africa is in a peculiarly difficult situation because of the multiplicity of its languages, the small number of speakers which can be claimed by the great bulk of them, the usual lack of a precolonial script for the sub-Saharan languages, and the absence, in most countries, of any one language whose predominance makes it the natural national language. It is said, for example, that there are two hundred and fifty languages in Nigeria, and, even if a great many of these could be written off as minimally significant, the country is still left with an intolerable multiplicity of tongues and nothing acceptable as a lingua franca except the alien, imperial English.[20] To adopt a European

[20] Nigerian independence brought forth pleas for the adoption of a Nigerian national language to meet the just claims of Nigerian pride and to make it possible to express the national essence. See, for example, Nkechi Ajarchukwu, "In Quest of National Language After Independence," *West African Pilot* September 30, 1960; C.S. Ola, "Now is the Time for One Language," *Daily Express* (Lagos), September 30, 1960.

language as the official working language of a country is to complicate immensely the educational system and to maintain, for a long time, the large gap which separates the Western-educated elite who speak, for a great part of their life, the alien language from the mass of the people who are familiar only with the vernacular; but, with the rarest of exceptions, the European language is the only one available. Although pleas have also been made for the study and teaching of African languages, it is significant that the first All African Peoples Conference, which met in Accra in 1958, should have called for the teaching of English in the secondary schools of French-speaking territories and vice versa "for the purpose of promoting intercourse among Africans on a continental basis." [21]

At many points, highly suggestive contrasts and comparisons can be drawn between Africa and India, itself a subcontinent with a large number of peoples, languages, traditions, cultures, and a population far larger than that of Africa. On the linguistic score, it is arguable that Africa, despite the great number of its languages, has an advantage over India in that it is not generally threatened by the spread of education in the vernacular which might disrupt a still tenuous national unity. In the case of India, where the country is divided into provinces on the basis of the linguistic communities (a number of which have tens of millions of speakers and can look back to established cultures and histories), it is by no means inconceivable that local nationalisms might arise to challenge the solidarity of the Indian nation. In Africa, unless tribalism reasserts itself to a wholly unexpected degree, it is highly unlikely that education in the vernaculars will build up communities which might turn to political separatism with a linguistic base.

Religion is of almost as little use as language in serving as the inner cement for African nations. The traditional African religions, which have retained their hold in many areas, may have had some basic points of philosophical or cosmological identity, but they were disparate and in no way linked to one

[21] Colin Legum, *op. cit.*, p. 231.

another. Both Islam and Christianity in their various sects and manifestations have penetrated deep into Africa, and a number of separatist African variants of them have appeared in one or another country. The animosities of Catholic and Protestant have translated themselves to Africa, finding political expression in Uganda, for example, and the brotherhood of all Moslems has not broken down the ethnic separatism of, say, the Hausa-Fulani in Nigeria in relation to the Yorubas, who have turned to Islam. In all probability, however, a more or less solidly Moslem country, such as the Somali Republic, could make the best use of religion in its nation-building. Elsewhere, religion is more likely to be a cause of division than a rallying point.

Because they are so young, inexperienced, and, in many instances, almost nonexistent, the military forces, which have played so large a role in other nations, cannot be expected to be of much significance in Africa for some time to come. However, the mere presence of national armed forces and the membership in them of young men from all sections and strata of the country have a significant effect in promoting national awareness, and the officer corps is likely to be strongly nationalist in outlook. Having achieved sovereignty, African states will surely achieve armaments as well, and it is only reasonable to assume that in a number of them the familiar pattern of military takeover in time of trouble (already put to use in the Sudan) will be repeated in due course.

A prime need for the building of a sense of national community in the new states is that at least a substantial segment of the people come to feel that their vital interests are linked with the state and that their well-being is enhanced by membership in it. The nation-state must be made to appear as the source of good and desirable things. A superficial bridging of the gap between the new state and the traditional societies can, no doubt, be accomplished by the adoption of such ceremonial forms as drums, dancing, and the use of traditional dress, as well as by seeking to equate the position of the political leader with that of the chief. The existence of the state itself, operating in a similar fashion for all its people and setting the law under which they live, must increasingly impress upon its members the fact that they constitute an entity distinct from that across the frontiers.

Insofar as programs are being translated into reality, the states are already being fully used by the dominant party leaders, who, uninhibited by scruples of *laissez faire* and free enterprise, see them as central instruments for nation-building and the attainment of national goals. Economic planning can be employed as a deliberate means of achieving a social mobilization which will draw people into the national community in the framework of what is frequently given the loose, but attractive, label of African Socialism. As economic and social development advances and as the means of transportation and communication are elaborated, a national economy begins to take shape; not only does this economy build up vested interests binding particular individuals and groups to the existing order, but also, in principle, gives everyone a stake in the maintenance of national strength and unity. Those formerly tied to a locality and clan are given a new national mobility and move into a money economy.

It is easy to conceive the ideal which seems so widely prevalent in Africa—a national mass party which reaches every corner of the country, a national state which implements the party's will and represents the country abroad, a national educational system which strengthens and disseminates the national culture, a national army to ward off the enemies within and without and a national economy to provide a popular well-being. To translate the ideal into practice—granted that it wins African acceptance—is a very different matter.

Building
the Newest Nations:
Short-Run
Strategies and
Long-Run Problems

8

William J. Foltz

As the preceding chapters suggest, building a nation is an exceedingly difficult and long task. Whether or not one accepts Professor Strayer's prediction of "an endless round of coups, conquests, revolutions, and wars," it is evident that the so-called "new nations" that have gained independence since World War II have only begun the arduous path to achieving viable and stable national existence. Indeed, as Professor Scott has shown, more than a century of independent existence has not sufficed to give the people of Latin America fully meaningful national identities. Professor Friedrich's suggestion that an integrated national identity may be too ambitious a goal for the new nations emphasizes, as do the leaders of these countries themselves, that their immediate task is the establishment of a strong governmental apparatus able to serve and control the population. The old argument over the priority of state or nation is being resolved by these countries' leaders in favor of first building the state as an instrument to bring about the nation.

As Professor Merritt's study of the American experience shows, however, obtaining even the sort of cooperation necessary for the regular functioning of a state apparatus may be dependent on the prior establishment of a strong sense of common identity and a common outlook among the "politically relevant strata" of a society on a wide variety of issues. A glance around today's globe suffices to show, however, that in many new states forceful governmental structures have been established that do not approach the level of internal communication and mutual comprehension of the thirteen American colonies on the eve of the Revolution. The problem here, it seems to me, is the composition and extent of the "politically relevant strata." A large proportion of the eighteenth-century American population not only possessed the skills requisite for participation in political decision-making, but also energetically insisted on such participation. Few rural hamlets were so small or isolated that they did not contain one voice whose words had to be reckoned with at some distant center of government. In contrast, most of the nations that have achieved their independence since World War II have had what is, from a short-range point of view at least, the good fortune to possess a narrowly constricted and homogeneous set of politically relevant strata. Furthermore, the large gap separating these people from the masses has permitted them to maintain themselves as a stable and nearly self-sufficient political elite during the most trying periods of political transition.

In most cases, this is not a gap of inherited traditional status, but one of modern achievement, most significantly educational achievement.[1] This, if anything, makes the gap more permanent, for ascribed status distinctions can sometimes be abolished overnight for political purposes, but most of the population cannot be taught overnight, or even in a few generations, the skills necessary to participate meaningfully and effectively in politics. The gap is between those living in the modern world and participating in the crucial decisions of the political arena and those living essentially as did their ancestors, bereft not only of skills

[1] For a similar educational distinction of elite from mass, see Claude Tardits, *Porto Novo* (Paris: Mouton, 1958), p. 11.

for modern politics and other modern occupations, but, in some cases, of even a minimal sense of identity with political structures and the people animating them. Although this gap provides the greatest long-run challenge to those who would build an integrated nation, in the short run it has given the elite the great flexibility of maneuver that is necessary to seize and consolidate the power of the state.

The educational structures of the newest states tend to reinforce polarization between elite and mass. Typically, there exists a great mass of people with no or only primary education and then, at the other extreme, a small but significant number of people with university-level training. What is lacking are people educated to the intermediate high school and junior high levels that characterize the bulk of the population in most advanced societies.[2] The reason for this gap is, on the surface, a good one. Because of the lack of educational funds, students for post-primary education must be rigorously selected at the sixth grade level. Those that succeed are then pushed to the limit of their abilities, which may be very great indeed. Without a large intermediate sector of reasonably competent and educated mid-elites, however, complex issues of government and administration are not interpreted and transmitted throughout society in meaningful terms that the masses can easily grasp. At the top, issues are faced in all their complexity; at the bottom, they are grouped and boiled down to simple slogans—"Independence now!" "One man, one vote!" Issues cannot be meaningfully debated within the populace at large, and votes tend to become mere approving plebiscites.

If, in society as a whole, there are few individuals in everyday life prepared to interpret and relate the problems of the elite to the masses, there are also few institutions capable of bridging the

[2] In Ghana, for instance, only about 12 per cent of those finishing primary school are admitted to advanced secondary training. Similarly, in the Ivory Coast in 1957 "only 750 out of 5,739 who completed primary school continued their education." At least half of these then went on to university training. Both countries have recently taken steps to expand secondary education. See Ruth Sloan Associates, *The Educated African* (New York: Praeger, 1962), esp. pp. 334–340, 460–469.

119

gap. In most African, and some Asian countries, the single, mass political party (*parti unique*) has played this role and has been the primary means of bringing the masses into contact with the political culture and inducting individuals into political roles.[3] Where the political party apparatus has been strong and active, the greatest political acculturation of the masses has taken place, as a comparison of, say, Guinea with Upper Volta or Ghana with Sierra Leone would show. However, the limits of this political acculturation should be noted. The masses are, for the most part, still associated with the receiving end of the political order. As Professor Scott put it, they are still "subjects," and their participation is ideally limited to applause on cue and, at most, to sullen foot-dragging when changes appear to be for the worse. Since the single, mass political parties, more than formal governmental or purely social organizations, often seem to be the prime mediators between elite and mass, they may, as Professor Emerson suggests, hold out the best hope for building the newest nations. We shall, therefore, take a more thorough look at their past successes and future possibilities.

Most of the currently ruling political parties in the newest states grew up under the late colonial regimes as instruments for attaining national independence. Particularly in the British and French colonial empires, the single, mass parties were singularly successful in leading the way to independence and quickly consolidating control over the government and administrative apparatuses once independence was achieved. The strength and success of these parties have rested on four principal factors. First, in "Independence!" they had a rallying cry of universal appeal. Typically, in any competitive party situation, the party that first proclaimed, "Freedom now," "Uhuru," or "N'dépendence" ended up on top once it had made itself the recognized spokesman for the feelings of vague revolt and common identity that usually

[3] "The *parti unique* is both an elite and a link. . . . The *parti unique* has as a goal to forge new elites, to create a new governing class, to unite and train political leaders capable of organizing the country, for the masses cannot govern themselves. . . . The party establishes a direct and permanent contact between [the political elite] and the country." Maurice Duverger, *Les Partis politiques* (Paris: Armand Colin, 1958), p. 288.

make up modern nationalism in the underdeveloped countries. Its espousal of national independence provided a focus around which both elite and mass could unite. Second, the single, mass party usually included virtually all the modern elite. These men were united by ties of personal friendship, frequently reinforced by common educational and agitational experiences and by dedication to the nationalist cause. Those members of the modern elite who did not join the mass party initially were generally co-opted at a later date or were so compromised by association with the colonial administration that they were ineffective as opposition leaders. Third, because of the dominance of the nationalist issue and because of the general lack of other modern structures, the single political party had no serious competition from other modern associations as a focus for popular loyalties. Finally, the single, mass party was generally well organized. The conditions of the political struggle and the dedication of the top elite to the party as the prime instrument of political change led the elite to give the major portion of their energies and resources to building a solid, responsive organization capable of disciplined action in response to directives from the top and able to ferret out and exploit feelings of dissatisfaction among the masses for political ends. The mass party became the framework within which ethnic, caste, and regional differences among the population at large could be submerged in the search for a common goal. It both embodied and promoted a preliminary sense of national unity and identity.

But winning independence, although it may be a necessary condition, is only the first and perhaps easiest step in building a nation. The new state apparatus must then be solidly implanted and extended, and the loyalty of the people to a stable governing regime, not to an agitational opposition movement, must be assured. However, the very factors making the mass party such an effective tool in the struggle for independence and permitting it to take over governmental power may be weakened by the day-to-day exercise of governmental responsibilities and by the nation-building process itself. Once formal independence is won, the unifying slogan of "Independence" has lost its magic force, and it is unlikely that anything quite so dramatic and effective can be found to replace it. Defending a revolution is always a less exciting and more onerous task than making it. Frequently, newly independent states seize on a new derivative slogan or goal to replace "independence" as a means of unifying both elite and mass. These secondary goals have frequently involved transforming the world outside the state to bring it more into line with the desires and presumed advantages of the new state, thus symbolically continuing the movement of independence. Such movements have sometimes, but not always, sought to export a national revolution or, as in Africa recently, to continue the independence movement to areas not yet favored by an enlightened colonial master. Of the same sort are the many irredentist movements designed to annex a lost or related territory or region, as, for example, the recent disputes between Morocco and Mauritania or Ghana and Togo. With such direct extensions of the goal of "national independence," governments frequently may promote a regional or federal unity movement of some sort, which may seek to reactivate popular emotions by redirecting them toward a greater whole. Pan-Africanism and Pan-Arabism are well-known examples.

Although turning to the outside world may provoke as strong an emotional yearning for unity as did the simpler search for national political unity and independence formerly, it may, in the short run, simply dilute or confuse more specific national sentiment. To the degree that it makes the success of the territorial nationalist movement dependent on that of a greater whole, it may in the long run succeed only in calling into question the worth of the national regime when the larger unity proves unrealizable.

The new state may try to unite its people by focusing animosities and frustrations on some external enemy, just as the nationalist movement focused its resentments on the colonial power or previous ruling class. To this end, the term "neocolonialism" has recently been invented. Those who brandish "neocolonialism" as a political slogan warn against continued domination by the former masters, now presumably operating behind the scenes through control of indigenous puppets and the new state's economy. Moise Tshombe's regime in Katanga is generally presented as the most blatant example of neocolonialism, but domestic difficulties in the most anti-imperialist states may be blamed on secret neocolonialists. "Neocolonialism" as a political slogan does have the great advantage of being almost universally applicable. By definition, neocolonialism operates behind the scenes, so virtually anything can be blamed on it. At the same time, however, its very ethereality means that neocolonialism is not directly experienced by the man in the street as was foreign political or military control, and it may, thereby, be a less effective political slogan.

Finally, the new state may choose some purely internal, non-symbolic goal to replace national independence as a national rallying cry. The "battle for economic development" is the most common and significant such goal today, as one would expect. However praiseworthy economic development may be as a national goal and however important it may be for long-term nation-building, it is still not likely to have the political potency of "independence." No matter how it is explained to them, few people are likely to make voluntarily and happily the sacrifices required in order to increase the gross national product by 3 per cent per annum or whatever else the goal might be. Furthermore, to the extent that most of the new states are primarily agricultural countries, the new regimes are obliged to earn precious domestic developmental capital from the sweat of peasantry fulfilling and overfulfilling their quotas. Thus, the first results of the drive for economic development may be a tougher lot for the very people for whom the new regime was brought into power—a fact which is unlikely to increase the masses' esteem for the regime.

As the mass party in the newly independent state is deprived of "independence" as a national rallying cry, so, too, its organization may suffer once it has passed from systematic opposition to coping with the demands of day-to-day administration. Talents that once were available for the crucial work of party organization may now be preoccupied with running a ministry or government bureau. This will be particularly true where the conditions under which independence was obtained led to the withdrawal of European advisors and technicians and threw the whole technical and administrative burden on the shoulders of the young indigenous politicians. Unless new sources of loyal organizational and administrative talents can be found immediately, the party's organization—and, therefore, the major link between the regime and the masses—is likely to be weakened.

If, in the days of nationalist agitation for independence, the mass party provided the unique and inclusive instrument for popular political participation, this is not likely to be the case after independence is attained. Governing an independent country requires indigenous participation in a great variety of new, formally constituted units. A civil service and national army are only the minimal, though most essential, organizations that must be staffed. Although these, like the governmental apparatus, will formally be brought under the control of the mass party, they can be expected to become new focuses of loyalty and to develop new goals, priorities, and methods that are at variance with those of the mass party. With increased specialization of function, the elite will share fewer and fewer common perspectives and experiences and will develop personal and group interests that could well produce internal scissions that were absent when the mass political party was the single organ of political expression, participation, and planning.

Of course, in theory, the new organizations should complement the mass party as the means of bridging the gap between the elite and the masses. However, if a struggle for influence pitting army or administration against the party develops, the very contacts of the new organizations with the masses may serve to divide the people more deeply than they were when only the party undertook to link them with the realm of modern politics. This will be particularly the case in cultures where personal leadership is important, and an army general, top administrator, or cabinet minister may build a personal following among the population at large.

The dispersion of leadership talents and the competition

of different decision-making units may be further accentuated if economic development is given top priority by the ruling elite. It is in part to prevent the creation of autonomous domestic decision-making units with a basis of economic power that many new states have refused to expand the private sector of the economy, even when such expansion would clearly contribute to economic development. It is not, in this sense, paradoxical that one of the most "revolutionary" new states, Guinea, should have tried repressing all domestic free enterprise while signing major contracts for exploitation of her natural resources with a consortium of Western private concerns. As the Guineans saw it, the foreigners would remain outside the sphere of domestic politics, but any Guinean private enterprise might augment fissiparous tendencies in the body politic. Elsewhere in the new states, governments have promoted or insisted upon partnership with private capital in all major economic enterprises to ensure the regime's control over the decisions and credit for any success.

Even where economic planning and execution remain firmly in governmental hands, however, one may expect to find a new center of power created in the planning ministry, allied or not allied with the civil service against the party and regime. This would seem almost inevitable if economic development is to be given serious priority. On almost every level, the demands of economic efficiency are sure to conflict at some point with the demands of political expediency or orthodoxy. Since their independence, Indonesia and Ghana have continually faced such conflicts. This type of conflict was illustrated most dramatically in December, 1962, when the Senegalese party leaders felt obliged to remove the prime minister and dismantle the planning and administrative apparatus under his control when they seemed to threaten party primacy.

But this is a realm in which the single-party regime must tread lightly, for the outcome of the struggle for pre-eminence is not at all foreordained. The further development has gone, the more opposition the regime will arouse among the technically oriented younger elites if the party chooses to slow down or stop change as a means of maintaining political control. This has, of course, been particularly the case in Burma, Pakistan, and Sudan, where technical military elites have seized power from the politicians. As Professor Wilson points out in his chapter, the military may have its own way of building a nation with or without the participation of a party apparatus.

In a somewhat broader perspective, the implementation of rapid economic and social change and, in particular, of educational development can open a whole range of new problems centered around controlling the burgeoning new elites. In part this is simply a qualitative problem. The promising young men who are trained after independence has been won will have quite different associations, perceptions, and preoccupations from those of their elders of the nationalist generation. Furthermore, since the nationalist generation is likely to come into power around age forty at the most, it is unlikely to fade from the scene so quickly as the new generation would like. On the other hand, the new generation is likely to have more formal education than its elders, particularly in technical domains. Also, since it will in all probability be trained abroad for the most part, it will escape the direct influence of the single-party regime during the crucial formative years of adolescence. It is not surprising that a recent survey of African students in France revealed that 63 per cent considered themselves in serious conflict with their governments.[4] After their return to home, one would naturally expect these young men to side with one of the alternative loci of power in the country, particularly if they are blocked, as they must be if the single-party regime's continuity is to be maintained, in their attempt to accede immediately to posts of high responsibility and power. This clash of interests was emphasized in Guinea in 1962, when several of the young intellectuals sought to impose their political vision on the single-party regime. In a direct confrontation, the party leaders jailed the intellectual leaders, recalled Guinean students from abroad, locked rebellious *lycée* students in their school, sent in the loyal party youth group, made up of the educationally underprivileged, to teach the students a les-

[4] J. P. N'Diaye, *Enquête sur les étudiants noirs en France* (Paris: Réalités Africaines, 1962), p. 223.

son—something they did with considerable gusto. In this state, as in other new states, the regime has, in times of stress, tended to fall back on loyal, if uneducated, political cadres rather than on the new elites. Although this may be a proper response to a short-run problem, it may have adverse effects on long-run political development.

But the rapid creation of new elites has a quantitative dimension of equal importance. It is one thing to integrate smoothly ten, twenty, or fifty returning students a year into the single-party regime and to inculcate in them the established political values and perceptions, but it is quite another to integrate a hundred or five hundred, particularly if they cannot be given the positions of top leadership to which they aspire because their fathers or older brothers are reluctant to step down. Without the clear necessity of pulling together to achieve independence and with a wider range of choices than faced the nationalist generation, these young men are unlikely to melt quietly into the previously established single-party regime. Nor are they so likely as were their elders to make the attempt to bridge the gap separating them from the masses, since by doing so they may only diminish the distinctiveness of their personal elite position without necessarily gaining corresponding political advantage. With no provisions for a loyal open opposition, a disloyal covert opposition may seem the only choice.

The emphasis on rapid social and economic change also poses problems for the single-party state on the level of the masses. If, through economic and social planning, one increases the rate of popular mobilization,[5] one also increases the demands made on the government. Although this mobilization is essential for building national sentiment among the masses, it may also threaten the regime if the government cannot keep pace with the new demands. Although in most cases this social mobilization was begun under the colonial regime, the colonial power was

[5] On the concept of mobilization, see Karl W. Deutsch, "Social Mobilization and Political Development," *American Political Science Review*, LV, No. 3 (1961), 493–514.

WILLIAM J. FOLTZ

seldom attentive to these demands, even if it had been capable of
responding. The nationalist single-party movement learned to be
attentive to the masses' demands and used the colonial regime's
reluctance to respond as an argument for seizing power. The independent single-party regime may continue to be attentive, but
it is unlikely to possess the resources for responding effectively
if mobilization proceeds at too great a pace. Alternatively, it may
emphasize building an effective response capability by giving the
younger technical elites their head and playing down the political party structure. But, in doing this, it may end by making
the new regime less well attuned to the immediate wants of the
mobilized and dissatisfied masses, thereby inadvertently re-creat-
ing a situation analogous to that of the colonial era. A rigid
new bureaucracy, even if technically competent and filled with
good intentions, may open the possibility of new popular revolts
led, perhaps, by disaffected politicians of the older nationalist
generation who have maintained their links with the masses. Such
a conflict between a distant technical bureaucracy and politicians
of the nationalist generation has been particularly acute in the
new states where the military has seized power.[6]

The new states will increasingly be obliged to make some
hard long-range decisions for which the experience and habits
acquired in the period of nationalist agitation will provide little
guidance. Stated most baldly, the polar choices open to the new
states hold terrors equal to those of Scylla and Charybdis. At
one extreme, a state may choose to ride the tiger of exacerbated
pluralism and possible internal strife and disintegration, and, at
the other extreme, it may choose to restrain social and economic
change to a level that can be handled by the existing political
structures. Similarly, the new regimes face a choice between transforming themselves completely to the profit of the new post-
nationalist elites, with the attendant danger of losing political at-
tentiveness to popular demands and what remains of the prestige
(and personnel) of the nationalist movement, and, on the other

[6] See Lucian W. Pye, "The Army in Burmese Politics," in John J. Johnson,
ed., *The Role of the Military in Underdeveloped Countries* (Princeton:
Princeton University Press, 1962), pp. 231–251.

hand, constricting access to the political elite, with the possibilities of political stagnation and turning the younger generation of elites against the regime.

It is difficult to predict at what point a given regime will succeed in striking a balance between these extremes. In general, it would seem that the closer to either extreme a regime comes, the poorer its chance of maintaining political integrity and eventually building a nation. Long-run pressures, especially those of an economic sort, would seem to be on the side of a more pluralist political process permitting entry of at least some new elites into the legitimate political arena and associating at least some newly mobilized sectors of the population with these elites through structures more or less outside the existing single-party framework. If this increase in political and social pluralism does not seriously weaken central governmental authority and create focuses of loyalty that challenge the legitimacy of the nation itself, rather than just a particular group of leaders or a specific policy, the nation-building process should be considerably advanced. For such a dynamic compromise to be maintained over the long run, the existing regime in most of the newest states must first feel itself secure enough from disruptive internal and external pressures to permit it to accept the necessary loosening of direct political control. At least in the short run, most such regimes will require absolute loyalty from new elites and acquiescence from the population at large, if only as evidence that the state is firmly enough established to permit the nation to be built.

Ensuring the short-run stability of the new states has led many regimes into practices which appear particularly objectionable to most people with a liberal democratic tradition. The "cult of personality" built around the national hero, the mouthing of seemingly senseless revolutionary slogans after the apparent revolution has been won, and the suppression of opposition groups and leaders are among the practices most commonly noted in the Western press. Although the disadvantages of these practices are readily apparent—at least to the outside observer with no immediate policy responsibilities—they may also serve useful functions in permitting the regimes to survive the initial period of building the state and make a successful transition to building a nation. Popular identification with a national hero and commitment to a revolutionary program, whether or not confined purely to the verbal level, both have the advantage of dissociating the state from a particular group of individuals making up the nationalist regime and permitting the people at large or new elites to serve and identify with a specific leader or set of policies. The national hero can retain not only the loyalty of the mass of the people, who are perhaps annoyed at specific government agents for specific causes, but can also go against his own lieutenants and bring new elites into the regime. Both Nasser and Nkrumah have used their positions in this way. Similarly, concentration on some sort of ideology, even if only symbolic, permits popular recognition of particular governmental functions above and beyond the specific individuals fulfilling those functions. At the same time, it holds up a national goal for younger elites to follow, and, by their acceptance of such a goal, they may more easily be brought into smoothly-functioning relationships with the incumbent elite.

Finally, the suppression of opposition leaders, and even of some of the new elites, may, with luck, permit the new states to get over the most trying period of postrevolutionary letdown without a collapse of the ruling regime, either through internal bickering or outside attacks. To the extent that the new state concentrates on building a more continuous educational system at home and to the extent that it has time to indoctrinate the younger elites in loyalty to the new political order, succeeding elites should pose fewer problems to the regime than does the immediate postrevolutionary generation.

The ability of the newest states to grow out of their initial periods of restrictive consolidation of power and into a more balanced society-wide pattern of national growth will depend in part on the willingness of the leaders to envisage fundamental revisions in the relations between the regime and its people and also on whether the adoption of less restrictive policies brings with it sufficient rewards to make the risk of pluralism worth taking. Certainly, if economic and social development seem impossible no matter what course of action is adopted or if the nations in the best position to assist a new state turn a deaf ear to a regime's initial pleas for assistance, the sterile pattern of repression, stagnation, and revolt will become the lot of most states. Instead of profiting from the West's arduous history of nation-building, the newest nations may then be condemned to repeat the long apprenticeship of "coups, conquests, revolutions, and wars" before they, too, evolve viable national societies.

A Selection
of Recent Works
on Nation-Building

BIBLIOGRAPHY

Donald J. Puchala

Bibliographies

Deutsch, K. W. *Interdisciplinary Bibliography on Nationalism, 1935–1953*. Cambridge, Mass.: Technology Press of the Massachusetts Institute of Technology, 1956.

Pinson, K. S. *A Bibliographical Introduction to Nationalism.* New York: Columbia University Press, 1935.

Smith, B. L., Lasswell, H. D., and Casey, R. D. *Propaganda, Communication, and Public Opinion.* Princeton: Princeton University Press, 1946.

Smith, B. L., and Smith, C. M. *International Communication and Political Opinion.* Princeton: Princeton University Press, 1956.

General and Theoretical Books

Almond, G. A., and Coleman, J. S. *The Politics of Developing Areas.* Princeton: Princeton University Press, 1960.

Andrzejewski, S. *Military Organization and Society.* London: Routledge and Kegan Paul Ltd., 1954.

Carr, E. H. *Nationalism and After.* New York: The Macmillan Company, 1945.

Claude, I. L. *National Minorities.* Cambridge, Mass.: Harvard University Press, 1955.

Deutsch, K. W. *Nationalism and Social Communication: An Inquiry into the Foundation of Nationality.* Cambridge, Mass., and New York: Massachusetts Institute of Technology Press and John Wiley and Sons, Inc., 1953.

——— *Political Community at the International Level.* Garden City, N.Y.: Doubleday and Company, Inc., 1954.

——— *et al. Political Community and the North Atlantic Area.* Princeton: Princeton University Press, 1957.

Earle, E. M. (ed.) *Nationalism and Internationalism.* New York: Columbia University Press, 1950.

Emerson, R. *From Empire to Nation.* Cambridge, Mass.: Harvard University Press, 1960.

Fesler, J. W. *Area and Administration.* University, Ala.: University of Alabama Press, 1949.

Guetzkow, H. *Multiple Loyalties: Theoretical Approach to a Problem in International Organization.* The Center for Research on World Political Institutions, Woodrow Wilson School of Public and International Affairs, Princeton: Princeton University Press, 1955.

Haskins, C. P. *Of Societies and Men*. New York: W. W. Norton & Company, Inc., 1951.

Hayes, C. J. *Nationalism: A Religion*. New York: The Macmillan Company, 1960.

Kaplan, M. A. *The Revolution in World Politics*. New York: John Wiley & Sons, Inc., 1962.

Kautsky, J. H. *Political Change in Underdeveloped Countries: Nationalism and Communism*. New York: John Wiley & Sons, Inc., 1962.

Kohn, H. *Nationalism: Its Meaning and History*. Princeton: D. Van Nostrand Company, Inc., 1955.

———— *The Idea of Nationalism*. New York: The Macmillan Company, 1961.

———— *Prophets and Peoples; Studies in Nineteenth Century Nationalism*. New York: The Macmillan Company, 1957.

Lasswell, H. D., *World Politics and Personal Insecurity*. Glencoe, Ill.: The Free Press, 1950.

———— *The World Revolution of Our Time*. Stanford, Calif.: Stanford University Press, 1951.

Lerner, D. *The Passing of Traditional Society*. Glencoe, Ill.: The Free Press, 1958.

Maass, A. (ed.) *Area and Power*. Glencoe, Ill.: The Free Press, 1959.

Millikan, M. F., and Blackmer, D. L. M. *The Emerging Nations: Their Growth and United States Policy*. Boston and Toronto: Little Brown & Company, 1961.

Plamenatz, J. P. *On Alien Rule and Self-Government*. London: Longmans, 1960.

Pye, L. W. *Communication and Political Development*. Princeton: Princeton University Press, 1963.

———— *Politics, Personality and Nation Building*. New Haven: Yale University Press, 1962.

Shafer, B. C. *Nationalism, Myth and Reality*. New York: Harcourt Brace and Company, 1955.

Sigmund, P. E., Jr. (ed.) *The Ideologies of the Developing Nations*. New York: Frederick A. Praeger, Inc., 1963.

Whitaker, U. G. *Nationalism and International Progress*. San Francisco: Chandler Publishing Company, 1961.

Znaniecki, F. *Modern Nationalities, A Sociological Study*. Urbana, Ill.: University of Illinois Press, 1952.

General and Theoretical Articles

Alker, H. R., Jr. "An IBM 709 Program for the Gross Analysis of Transaction Flows." *Behavioral Science*, October 1962.

Apter, D. E. "Nationalism, Government and Economic Growth," *Economic Development and Cultural Change*, January 1959.

Ashford, D. E. "Patterns of Consensus in Developing Countries," *American Behavioral Scientist*, April 1961.

Beloff, M. "Nationalism in the Western World," *Western World*, January 1959.

Cutright, P. "National Political Development: Measurement and Analysis." *American Sociological Review*, February 1962.

Davies, J. C. "Toward a Theory of Revolution." *American Sociological Review*, February 1962.

Deutsch, K. W. "The Growth of Nations: Some Recurrent Patterns of Political and Social Integration," *World Politics*, January 1953.

———— "Social Mobilization and Political Development," *American Political Science Review*, September 1961.

Emerson, R. "Nationalism and Political Development," *Journal of Politics*, February 1960.

Hoover Institution on War, Revolution and Peace. *A Conference on the Social Sciences in Historical Study, June 20–22, 1957,* Stanford, Calif.: Stanford University, 1957 (multigraphed).

Lerner, D. "Communications Systems and Social Systems: A Statistical Exploration in History and Policy," *Behavioral Science,* March 1959.

Lipset, S. M. "Some Social Requisites of Democracy: Economic Development and Political Legitimacy," *American Political Science Review,* March 1959.

Mehden, F. R. van der. "Party Development in Newly Independent States," *Social Science,* June 1959.

Parkinson, F. "Social Dynamics of Underdeveloped Countries," *Yearbook of World Affairs,* 1960.

Savage, R. I., and Deutsch, K. W. "A Statistical Model of the Gross Analysis of Transaction Flows." *Econometrica,* July 1960.

Shannon, L., "Socio-Economic Development and Political Status," *Social Problems,* Fall 1959.

———— "Is Level of Development Related to Capacity for Self-Government?" *The American Journal of Economics and Sociology,* July 1958.

Shils, E. "The Intellectuals in the Political Development of New States," *Social Science,* June 1959.

Africa: Books

Apter, D. E. *Ghana in Transition*. New York: Atheneum, 1962.

——— *The Political Kingdom in Uganda; A Study in Bureaucratic Nationalism*. Princeton: Princeton University Press, 1961.

Bourret, F. M. *Ghana: The Road to Independence 1919–1957*. Stanford, Calif.: Stanford University Press, 1960.

Bretton, H. L. *Power and Stability in Nigeria*. New York: Frederick A. Praeger, Inc., 1962.

Carter, G. (ed.) *African One-Party States*. Ithaca, N.Y.: Cornell University Press, 1960.

Carter, G. *Independence for Africa*. New York: Frederick A. Praeger, 1960.

Carter, G., and Brown, W. (ed.) *Transition in Africa: Studies in Political Adaptation*. Boston: Boston University Press, 1958.

Coleman, J. S. *Nigeria: Background to Nationalism*. Berkeley: University of California Press, 1958.

Doob, L. *Communication in Africa: A Search for Boundaries*. New Haven: Yale University Press, 1961.

Foltz, W. J. *From French West Africa to the Mali Federation*. Forthcoming, 1963.

Hodgkin, T. *African Political Parties*. Baltimore: Penguin Books Inc., 1961.

——— *Nationalism in Colonial Africa*. New York: New York University Press, 1956.

Kimble, G. H. T. *Tropical Africa*. New York: The Twentieth Century Fund, 1960.

N'Diaye, J. P. *Enquête sur les étudiants noirs en France.* Paris: Réalités Africaines, 1962.

Perham, M. *The Colonial Reckoning.* New York: Alfred A. Knopf, 1962.

Richards, A. I. (ed.) *East African Chiefs: A Study of Political Development in Some Uganda and Tanganyika Tribes.* London: Faber and Faber, 1960.

Spiro, H. J. *Politics in Africa.* Englewood Cliffs, N.J.: Prentice-Hall, Inc., 1962.

Wallerstein, I. *Africa: The Politics of Independence.* New York: Vintage Books, 1961.

Africa: Articles

Apter, D. "The Role of Traditionalism in the Political Modernization of Ghana and Uganda." *World Politics,* October 1960.

Berg, E. J. "The Economic Basis of Political Choice in French West Africa," *American Political Science Review,* June 1960.

Blumenfeld, Y. Y. "Tribalism vs. Nationalism in African Development," *Editorial Research Reports,* 1960.

Blundell, M. "Making a Nation in Kenya," *African Affairs,* July 1959.

British Survey, "Nigeria: The Building of a Nation," September 1960.

Chidzero, B. T. G. "African Nationalism in East and Central Africa," *International Affairs,* October 1960.

Decraene, P., "Independence et regroupements politiques en Afrique au sud du Sahara," *Revue Française de Science Politique,* December 1960.

Gordon, W. "In Newest Africa: Three Nationalisms Compete for its Emerging Peoples," *Nieman Reports,* 1959.

Guillemin, P. "La Structure des premiers gouvernements locaux en Afrique noire: contribution à l'étude d'un parlementarisme naissant," *Revue Française de Science Politique,* September 1959.

Hodgkin, T., and Schachter, R. "French Speaking West Africa in Transition," *International Conciliation,* May 1960.

Kilson, M. L., Jr. "Nationalism and Social Classes in British West Africa," *The Journal of Politics,* May 1958.

Kitchen, H. "The Sudan Transition," *Current History,* July 1959.

Laqueur, W. Z. "Communism and Nationalism in Tropical Africa," *Foreign Affairs,* July 1961.

Lemarchand, R. "The Limits of Self-Determination: The Case of Katanga," *American Political Science Review,* June 1962.

Mercier, P. "Political Life in the Urban Centers of Senegal: A Study of a Period of Transition," *PROD Translations,* June 1960.

Moreira, A. "Political Unity and the Status of Peoples," *African Affairs,* July 1960.

Nixon, C. P. "The Conflict of Nationalisms in South Africa," *World Politics,* October 1958.

Perham, M. "The Psychology of African Nationalism," *Optima,* March 1960.

Pratt, R. C. "Nationalism in Uganda," *Political Studies,* June 1961.

Schachter, R. "Single Party Systems in West Africa," *American Political Science Review,* June 1961.

DONALD J. PUCHALA

Sklar, R. L. "The Contribution of Tribalism to Nationalism in Western Nigeria," *Journal of Human Relations,* Spring and summer 1960.

Wallerstein, I. "Ethnicity and National Integration in West Africa," *Cahiers d'Études Africaines,* No. 3 (1960).

——— "How Seven States Were Born in Former French West Africa," *Africa Report,* December 1960.

Williams, D. "How Deep the Split in West Africa?" *Foreign Affairs,* October, 1961.

Zolberg, A. R. "Effets de la structure d'un parti politique sur l'intégration nationale," *Cahiers d'Études Africaines,* No. 3 (1960).

North Africa and Near East: Books

Ahmed, J. M. *The Intellectual Origins of Egyptian Nationalism.* New York: Oxford University Press, 1960.

Ashford, D. E. *Political Change in Morocco.* Princeton: Princeton University Press, 1961.

Brace, R., and Brace, J. *Ordeal in Algeria.* Princeton: D. Van Nostrand Company, Inc., 1958.

Gillespie, J. *Algeria: Rebellion and Revolution.* New York: Frederick A. Praeger, Inc., 1960.

Hahn, L. *North Africa: Nationalism to Nationhood.* Washington, D.C.: Public Affairs Press, 1960.

Lacouture, J., and Lacouture, S. *Egypt in Transition.* New York: Criterion Books, 1958.

Rustow, D. *Politics and Westernization in the Near East.* Princeton: Princeton University Press, 1956.

Safran, N. *Egypt in Search of Political Community*. Cambridge, Mass.: Harvard University Press, 1961.

Tillion, G. *France and Algeria, Complementary Enemies*. New York: A. A. Knopf, 1961.

North Africa and Near East: Articles

Ashford, D. E. "Patterns of Group Development in a New Nation: Morocco," *American Political Science Review*, June 1961.

Bernier, T. "Naissance d'un nationalisme arabe à Aden," *L'Afrique et l'Asie*, No. 4 (1958).

Carey, J. P. C., and Carey, A. G. "Libya: From Colony to Nation," *Foreign Policy Bulletin*, April 1, 1961.

Elwell-Sutton, L. P. "Nationalism and Neutralism in Iran," *The Middle East Journal*, Winter 1958.

Harari, M. "The Dynamics of Lebanese Nationalism," *Current History*, February 1959.

Lerner, D. "The Middle East: Human Meaning of Modernization," *Foreign Policy Bulletin*, March 1, 1959.

Lerner, D. and Robinson, R. D. "Swords and Ploughshares: the Turkish Army as a Modernizing Force," *World Politics*, October 1960.

Mughaizel, J. "Secularism and Arab Nationalism," *Middle East Forum*, December 1960.

Patai, R. "Nationalism in Jordan," *Current History*, February 1959.

Pranger, R. J. "Currents in Iranian Nationalism," *Current History*, February 1959.

Romeril, P. "Tunisian Nationalism," *Middle East Journal*, Spring 1960.

Rustow, D. A. "The Army and the Founding of the Turkish Republic," *World Politics*, July 1959.

Shepard, G. W. "Tunisia and Arab Nationalism," *Current History*, July 1959.

Sherman, A. V. "Turkey—A Case in Constructive Nationalism," *Commentary*, August 1960.

Twitchell, K. S. "Nationalism in Saudi Arabia," *Current History*, February 1959.

Zeidner, R. F. "Kurdish Nationalism and the New Iraq Government," *Middle East Affairs*, January 1959.

South and Southeast Asia, the Far East, and Pacific: Books

Brown, D. *Nationalism in Japan*. Berkeley: University of California Press, 1955.

Desai, A. R. *Recent Trends in Indian Nationalism*. Bombay: Popular Book Depot, 1960.

——— *Social Background of Indian Nationalism*. Bombay: Popular Book Depot, 1959.

Harrison, S. S. *India: the Most Dangerous Decades*. Princeton: Princeton University Press, 1960.

Johnson, C. A. *Chinese Peasant Nationalism*. Stanford, Calif.: Stanford University Press, 1962.

King, F. H. H. *The New Malayan Nation: A Study of Communalism and Nationalism*. New York: Institute of Pacific Relations, 1957.

Menon, V. *The Story of the Integration of the Indian States*. Bombay: Orient Longmans, 1956.

—— *The Transfer of Power in India*. Princeton: Princeton University Press, 1957.

Morris, I. *Nationalism and the Right Wing in Japan*. New York: Oxford University Press, 1960.

Pye, L. W. *The Spirit of Burmese Politics*. Center for International Studies, Cambridge, Mass.: Massachusetts Institute of Technology Press, 1959.

Sharma, J. S. *Indian National Congress, a Descriptive Bibliography of India's Struggle for Freedom*. Delhi: S. Chand & Company, 1959.

Smith, T. C. *The Agrarian Origins of Modern Japan*. Stanford, Calif.: Stanford University Press, 1959.

Tinker, H. *The Union of Burma: A Study of the First Year of Independence*. New York: Oxford University Press, 1957.

Weiner, M. *The Politics of Scarcity: Public Pressure and Political Response in India*. Chicago: University of Chicago Press, 1962.

Wertheim, W. F. *Indonesian Society in Transition*. The Hague and Bandung: W. Van Hoeve Ltd., 1956.

Wilson, D. *Politics in Thailand*. Ithaca, N.Y.: Cornell University Press, 1962.

South and Southeast Asia, The Far East, and Pacific: Articles

Binder, L. "Pakistan and Modern Islamic-Nationalist Theory," *The Middle East Journal*, Winter 1958.

Bondurant, J. "Regionalism vs. Provincialism: A Study in Problems of Indian National Unity," *Indian Press Digest* (Monograph Series), December 1958.

Bristol, J. E. "Nationalism and Nonviolence in India," *Fellowship*, September 1, 1959.

Dash, S. C. "Nature and Significance of Indian Nationalism," *Indian Journal of Political Science*, January-March 1958.

Kroef, J. M. van der. "Nationalism and Politics in West New Guinea," *Pacific Affairs*, Spring 1961.

——— "The Role of Islam in Indonesian Nationalism and Politics," *Western Political Quarterly*, March 1958.

Mehden, F. R. van der. "Marxism and Early Indonesian Islamic Nationalism," *Political Science Quarterly*, September 1958.

Rangnekar, D. K. "The Nationalist Revolution in Ceylon," *Pacific Affairs*, December 1960.

Spear, P. "From Colonial to Sovereign Status: Some Problems of Transition with Special Reference to India," *The Journal of Asian Studies*, August 1958.

Wriggins, W. H. "Impediments to Unity in New Nations: The Case of Ceylon," *American Political Science Review*, June 1961.

Latin America and the Caribbean: Books

Adams, R. N., *et al. Social Change in Latin America Today*. New York: Harper and Brothers, 1960.

Alexander, R. J. *Bolivian National Revolution*. New Brunswick, N.J.: Rutgers University Press, 1958.

Alexander, R. J., and Porter, C. O. *The Struggle for Democracy in Latin America*. New York: The Macmillan Company, 1961.

Ayearst, M. *The British West Indies, The Search for Self-Government*. New York: New York University Press, 1960.

Blanksten, G. *Ecuador: Constitutions and Caudillos.* Berkeley: University of California Press, 1951.

———— *Perón's Argentina.* Chicago: University of Chicago Press, 1953.

Bushnell, D. *The Santander Regime in Gran Colombia.* ("University of Delaware Monograph Series.") Newark, Del.: University of Delaware Press, 1954.

Fitzgibbon, R. A. *Uruguay: Portrait of a Democracy.* New Brunswick, N.J.: Rutgers University Press, 1956.

Fluharty, V. L. *Dance of the Millions: Military Rule and Social Revolutions in Colombia, 1930–1956.* Pittsburgh: University of Pittsburgh Press, 1957.

Hirschman, A. O. *Latin American Issues.* New York: The Twentieth Century Fund, 1961.

Johnson, J. J. *Political Change in Latin America.* Stanford, Calif.: Stanford University Press, 1961.

Lasso, G. P. *Problems of Democracy in Latin America.* Chapel Hill, N.C.: University of North Carolina Press, 1955.

Lieuwen, E. *Arms and Politics in Latin America.* New York: Frederick A. Praeger Inc., 1961.

Scott, R. E. *Mexican Government in Transition.* Urbana, Ill.: University of Illinois Press, 1959.

Szulc, T. *Twilight of the Tyrants.* New York: Henry Holt & Company, 1959.

Tannenbaum, F. *Mexico: The Struggle for Peace and Bread.* New York: Alfred A. Knopf, 1950.

Latin America and the Caribbean: Articles

Alexander, R. J. "Nationalism, Latin America's Predominant Ideology." *Journal of International Affairs,* Fall 1961.

Burr, R. M. (ed.) "Latin America's Nationalistic Revolutions," *The Annals of the American Academy of Political and Social Science,* March 1961.

Fitzgibbon, R. H. "Dictatorship and Democracy in Latin America." *International Affairs,* January 1960.

———— "What Price Latin American Armies?" *Virginia Quarterly Review,* Winter 1960.

Fitzgibbon, R. H., and Johnson, K. F. "Measurement of Latin American Political Change." *American Political Science Review,* September 1961.

Hadley, P. E. "Latin America: Retreat from Violence?" *Western Political Journal,* June 1958.

Johnson, J. J. "Whither the Latin American Middle Sectors?" *Virginia Quarterly Review,* Fall 1961.

Kling, M. "Towards a Theory of Power and Political Instability in Latin America." *Western Political Review,* March 1956.

Mecham, J. L. "Democracy and Dictatorship in Latin America." *Southwestern Social Science Quarterly,* December 1960.

Rippy, J. "Dictatorship and Democracy in Latin America." *Inter-American Economic Affairs,* Summer 1960.

The United States (historical): Books

Boorstin, D. J. *The Americans: The Colonial Experience.* New York: Random House, 1958.

Brant, 1. *James Madison the Nationalist, 1780–1787*. New York: The Bobbs-Merrill Company, 1948.

Bridenbaugh, C. *Cities in Revolt: Urban Life in America, 1743–1776*. New York: Alfred A. Knopf, 1955.

Curti, M. *The Roots of American Loyalty*. New York: Columbia University Press, 1948.

Kohn, H. *American Nationalism, an Interpretative Essay*. New York: The Macmillan Company, 1957.

Kraus, M. *Intercolonial Aspects of American Culture on the Eve of the Revolution, with Special Reference to the Northern Towns*. New York: Columbia University Press, 1928.

Merritt, R. *Symbols of American Community, 1735–1775*. Doctoral dissertation, Yale University, 1962, currently being prepared for press.

Morgan, E. S. *The Birth of the Republic, 1763–89*. Chicago: The University of Chicago Press, 1956.

Morison, S. E., and Commager, H. S. *The Growth of the American Republic*. New York: Oxford University Press, 1962.

Potter, D. M. *People of Plenty*. Chicago: The University of Chicago Press, 1954.

Van Doren, C. *The Great Rehearsal*. New York: Viking Press, 1948.

Wright, L. B. *The Atlantic Frontier*. Ithaca, N.Y.: Cornell University Press, 1951.

Europe (historical): Books

Coupland, R. *Welsh and Scottish Nationalism: A Study*. London: Collins Sons and Company, 1954.

Kann, R. A. *The Habsburg Empire: A Study in Integration and Disintegration*. New York: Frederick A. Praeger, 1951.

―――― *The Multinational Empire*. New York: Columbia University Press, 1950.

Kantorowicz, E. H. *The King's Two Bodies*. Princeton: Princeton University Press, 1957.

Kohn, H. *Nationalism and Liberty: The Swiss Example*. New York: The Macmillan Company, 1956.

―――― *The Mind of Germany; the Education of a Nation*. New York: Charles Scribners Sons, 1960.

Lindgren, R. *Norway-Sweden: Union, Disunion, Reunion*. Princeton: Princeton University Press, 1959.

Niebuhr, R. *The Structure of Nations and Empires*. New York: Charles Scribners Sons, 1959.

Weilenmann, H. *Pax Helvetica*. Erlenbach and Zürich: E. Rentsch, 1951.

Europe (historical): Articles

Deutsch, K. W. "The Trend of European Nationalism—The Language Aspect." *American Political Science Review*, June 1942.

Friedrich, C. J. "The Agricultural Basis of European Nationalism." *Public Opinion Quarterly*, April 1937.

Economic Aspects: Books

Aitken, H. G. *The State and Economic Growth*. New York: Social Science Research Council, 1959.

Balassa, B. *The Theory of Economic Integration*. Homewood, Ill.: Richard D. Irwin, Inc., 1961.

Becker, G. S. *The Economics of Discrimination*. Chicago: University of Chicago Press, 1957.

Isaac, J. *Economics of Migration.* London: K. Paul, Trench, Trubner & Company, 1947.

Kindleberger, C. P. *Economic Development.* New York: The McGraw-Hill Book Company, Inc., 1958.

———— *Foreign Trade and the National Economy.* New Haven: Yale University Press, 1962.

Kuznets, S. *Six Lectures on Economic Growth.* Glencoe, Ill.: The Free Press, 1959.

Meade, J. *The Theory of Customs Unions.* Amsterdam: North-Holland Publishing Company, 1955.

Myrdal, G. *Beyond the Welfare State.* New Haven: Yale University Press, 1960.

———— *An International Economy.* New York: Harper and Brothers, 1956.

———— *Rich Lands and Poor.* New York: Harper and Brothers, 1957.

Robinson, E. A. G. (ed.) *The Economic Consequences of the Size of Nations.* New York: St. Martin's Press, Inc., 1960.

Sannwald, R. F., and Stohler, J. *Economic Integration.* Princeton: Princeton University Press, 1959.

Viner, J. *The Customs Union Issue.* New York: Carnegie Endowment for International Peace, 1950.

Economic Aspects: Articles

Chenery, H. B. "Comparative Advantage and Development Policy." *American Economic Review,* March 1961.

Deutsch, K. W. "The Propensity to International Transactions." *Political Studies,* November 1960.

Deutsch, K. W., Bliss, C. I., and Eckstein, A. "Population, Sovereignty, and the Share of Foreign Trade." *Economic Development and Cultural Change,* July 1962.

Deutsch, K. W., and Eckstein, A. "National Industrialization and the Declining Share of the International Sector." *World Politics,* January 1961.

Deutsch, K. W., and Russett, B. M. "International Trade and Political Independence." *The American Behavioral Scientist,* March 1963.

Some
Recent Works
on Nation-Building,
1963-1966

BIBLIOGRAPHY

Bibliographies

Deutsch, Karl W., and Merritt, Richard L. *Nationalism: An Interdisciplinary Bibliography*. Cambridge: M.I.T. Press, publication scheduled 1966.

de Grazia, Alfred. *Universal Reference System*. Vol. 1, *International Affairs*. New York: Universal Reference System, 1965.

General and Theoretical Books

Almond, Gabriel A., and Pye, Lucian W., eds. *Comparative Political Culture*. Princeton: Princeton University Press, 1965.

Apter, David E. *The Politics of Modernization*. Chicago: University of Chicago Press, 1965.

Deutsch, Karl W. *Nationalism and Social Communication: An Inquiry into the Foundation of Nationality.* Revised edition, Cambridge: M.I.T. Press, 1966.

Doob, Leonard W. *Patriotism and Nationalism: Their Psychological Foundation.* New Haven: Yale University Press, 1964.

Etzioni, Amitai. *Political Unification: A Comparative Study of Leaders and Forces.* New York: Holt, Rinehart & Winston, 1965.

Friedrich, Carl J. *Man and His Government.* New York: McGraw-Hill, 1963. Especially Chapter 30, "State and Nation: Sovereignty and its Limits," pp. 547–566.

Geertz, Clifford, ed. *Old Societies and New States: The Quest for Modernity in Asia and Africa.* New York: The Free Press of Glencoe, 1963.

Haas, Ernst B. *Beyond the Nation-State: Functionalism and International Organization.* Stanford: Stanford University Press, 1964. Especially Chapter 14, "Functionalism, Nationalism and Historical Sociology," pp. 459–497.

Hartz, Louis. *The Founding of New Societies: Studies in the History of the United States, Latin America, South Africa, Canada and Australia.* With contributions by Kenneth D. McRae and others. New York: Harcourt, Brace & World, 1964.

Jacob, Philip E., and Toscano, James V., eds. *The Integration of Political Communities.* Philadelphia: Lippincott, 1964.

Kelman, Herbert, ed. *International Behavior: A Social-Psychological Analysis.* New York: Holt, Rinehart & Winston, 1965.

La Palombara, Joseph, ed. *Bureaucracy and Political Development.* Princeton: Princeton University Press, 1963.

Lemberg, Eugen. *Nationalismus.* Vol. 1, *Psychologie und Ge-*

schichte; Vol. 2, *Soziologie und politische Pädagogik.* Reinbek bei Hamburg: Rowohlt, 1964.

Lipset, Seymour Martin. *The First New Nation: The United States in Historical and Comparative Perspective.* New York: Basic Books, 1963.

Merritt, Richard L., and Rokkan, Stein, eds. *Comparing Nations: The Use of Quantitative Data in Cross-national Research.* New Haven: Yale University Press, 1965.

Organski, A. F. K. *The Stages of Political Development.* New York: Alfred A. Knopf, 1965.

Pye, Lucian W., ed. *Communication and Political Development.* Princeton: Princeton University Press, 1963.

Russett, Bruce M. *Community and Contention: Britain and America in the Twentieth Century.* Cambridge: M.I.T. Press, 1963. Especially Chapter 12, "Notes on a Theory of Integration," pp. 208–221.

Russett, Bruce M., *et al. World Handbook of Political and Social Indicators.* New Haven: Yale University Press, 1964.

Silvert, K. H., ed. *Expectant Peoples: Nationalism and Development.* New York: Random House, 1963.

General and Theoretical Articles

Almond, Gabriel A. "A Developmental Approach to Political Systems." *World Politics,* January 1965.

Cutright, Phillips. "National Political Development: Measurement and Analysis." *American Sociological Review,* April 1963.

Deutsch, Karl W., and Rieselbach, Leroy N. "Recent Trends in Political Theory and Political Philosophy." *The Annals of the American Academy of Political and Social Science,* July 1965.

Eisenstadt, S. N. "Modernization and Conditions of Sustained Growth." *World Politics,* July 1964.

Halpern, Manfred. "Toward Further Modernization of the Study of New Nations." Review Article. *World Politics,* October 1964.

Hughes, Everett C. "Race Relations and the Sociological Imagination." *American Sociological Review,* December 1963.

Huntington, Samuel P. "Political Development and Political Decay." *World Politics,* April 1965.

Lasswell, Harold D. "The Policy Sciences of Development." Review Article. *World Politics,* January 1965.

Packenham, Robert A. "Approaches to the Study of Political Development." Research Note. *World Politics,* October 1964.

Riggs, Fred W. "The Theory of Developing Polities." Review Article. *World Politics,* October 1963.

von Vorys, Karl, ed. "New Nations: The Problem of Political Development." *The Annals of the American Academy of Political and Social Science,* March 1965.

INDEX

ABDEL NASSER, GAMAL, 130
Absolutism, 53
Accra, 114
Acculturation:
  America, 15
  Europe, 15
  India, 15
  political, 120
ADAMS, R. N., 144
Affiliation, 34, 41, 53
  basis of aggregate, 37
  communal, 43
  personal, 34
  social, 38
Africa, 4, 8, 11–16, 27, 95–116
  boundaries, 14
  business groups in, 16
  changes, 5
  colonialism in, 98–112; *see also*
    Imperialism
  education, 14–15, 111–114

elites, 14
ethnic groups, 96
ideal in, 116
and India, 114
levels of community, 97
mass media, 15
military forces, 115
national identity, 104
nationalism, 1–2, 73, 95–97
nationalists, 16
one-party system, 106–111
Pan-Africanism, 97, 97 n.
partitioning, 100
peasants, 15, 123
plural societies, 109
and political identity, 96
political participation, 9–10
religion, 114–115
revolutions and, 110–111
and social will, 109
states of, 25

155

Cold War and, 85
communal, 49
European, 73
  modern, 17
  Western, 85
expansion of, 50–52
French, 55
goal of, and individual, 47–48
and groups, 6–7
loyalty to, 22–24
according to Machiavelli, 28
medieval, 49
minorities in, 9
modern, 30
monarchical, 28
"mosaic," 23–25
and nation, 23, 117, 129–130
new:
  and American colonies, 118
  and education, 118–119
  and mass parties, 120–121, 123–
    124, 126–128
  and political elite, 118–124
participation in, 48
pass, 52
and people, 49, 115–116
and *polis*, 29
and old political units, 25
power over, 6
and *regnum*, 17–18, 23
Roman model, 19
secular, 22
sovereignty, 76
splinter-, 23–25
territory of, 48–50
theory of, in Middle Ages, 20
and tribe, 6–7
unitary, 23–24
will that creates, 43, 46, 53–54
Statesman, 2–3
STOHLER, J., 149
STRAYER, JOSEPH R., 4, 10, 17–29,
  32, 117
Structure:

political, in colonial America,
  57–61
social, 84, 87
two-class, 87
Struggle, necessity of, 38
Subculture, political, in Mexico,
  82
Subjects, in Mexico, 81
Sudan, 11, 115, 125–126
SULZBACH, WALTER, 101
Supreme Allied Commanders, 60
SUTHERLAND, STELLA H., 62 n.
Sweden, 29
Switzerland, 53
  democracy, 10
  people, 7
Symbol analysis, 67–72
SZULC, TAD, 145

Tanganyika, 102, 108–109
TANNENBAUM, F., 145
TARDITS, CLAUDE, 118 n.
TELLENBACH, GERD, 8 n.
Territory, of state and people, 48–
  53
Terrorism, and revolutionary war,
  92
Thailand, 86–87, 92
TILLION, G., 141
TINKER, H., 143
Togo, 101, 122
TOURÉ, SÉKOU, 106, 108 n.
Trade, in colonial America, 61–62,
  66
Tradition, importance of, 112–113
Traditionals, in Mexico, 81
Traits, configuration of, 34, 43
Transactions, among American
  colonies, 57
Transportation, in colonial Amer-
  ica, 62
Tribalism, 4–8
  in Africa, 97–102, 105–107, 113–
    115

169

WRIGHT, L. B., 147
WROTH. LAWRENCE C., 64 n.

Yale Political Data Program, 12
Yale University, 56 n.
Yoruba, 98, 115

ZEIDNER, R. F., 142
ZENGER, JOHN PETER, 63
ZNANIECKI, F., 135
ZOLBERG, A. R., 107 n., 140